Whirlpool People

Deconstructing the Illusion of the Self

Ben Moores

Theatre Elliptical

Whirlpool People: Deconstructing the Illusion of the Self

For information contact:
3 Bailey View, Groby, Leicestershire, LE6 0FF
www.theatreelliptical.co.uk

Cover design by Sumit Sakar
ISBN: 978-1-7397734-0-3

First Edition: February 2022

Dedicated to the memory of

Caroline Cecilia Schrempft

1983-2019

CONTENTS

Introduction, summary and overview

Continuous Monism

This book is an exploration of ideas and research within science, philosophy, psychology, spirituality and shamanism, which reveal that the fundamental reality of the universe is one indivisible process. It concludes that the experience of ourselves, as separate and independent individuals is an illusion because we must be continuous with, and indivisible from the one process of the universe. It demonstrates that we all have an innate capacity to experience our true reality as a continuation of this process. It delves deeply into the consequences and implications of this capacity, with regard to love, creativity, politics, music, meditation, nature, psychedelics, ethics, morality, death, art, humour, dreams, suffering, trauma and more. The evidence is synthesised into a theory that I call 'continuous monism'. This theory maps out the interrelationship between the ideas that are presented, to offer a perspective that goes beyond our individual selves, and encompasses oneness.

This introduction contains many condensed ideas and brief

definitions for terminology. Therefore, these ideas may seem abstract, esoteric, or overly complicated at first. However, during the following chapters, as they are expressed in more detail, and simplified, they will become more concrete, easily understandable and applicable to the reality of our lives, and the experience of being a person.

The continuous universe

One of the foundations of continuous monism is the notion of the 'continuous universe'. This is the concept that the universe is one unified continuous process, that consists of all phenomena, including: objects, thoughts, people, events, locations, space and time, and flows as one inseparable unified singular entity. 'Continuous' is the key word because it conveys that the universe cannot consist of any separate fragmented parts. A fragmented part, by definition, would not be continuous with the whole universe. Therefore, if the universe is continuous, then a fragmented part would have to be separate from the rest of the universe, and this would be impossible. Moreover, for a fragmented part to exist, separate from all other parts, then there would have to be empty space in between each part, but empty space doesn't exist. Even the "empty space" in between planets and stars, which we call a vacuum, is filled with phenomena such as the gravitational field, the electromagnetic field, cosmic rays and trillions of quantum particles that constantly fluctuate in and out of existence.

The reason to use the word 'continuous' instead of 'connected' is because something that is made of connected parts can be made of separate fragmented parts, but the universe flows as one unified entity.

Throughout history there have been many theories that describe the notion of the continuous universe, and here are some examples of those ideas: 'Pantheism' is the belief that all reality is identical with divinity and God as the one true transcendent substance of the universe, that encompasses all things. Pantheism was popularised by the philosopher Spinoza in the seventeenth century who said:

> *"God is the indwelling and not the transient cause of all things."*

In terms of philosophy, pantheism is a monistic philosophy of the universe. The fundamental quality of monistic philosophies is that they attribute oneness or singleness to the universe, therefore, according to any monistic philosophy, the universe is ultimately one unified structure at the most fundamental primary level of reality. This is opposed to 'dualism', in the tradition of the French philosopher René Descartes, which states that the universe is split into the two realities of 'matter and consciousness' or 'mind and body'. Moreover, in dualism, these two realities are distinct and separable. Spinoza's concept of pantheism defines God as the totality of phenomena. It states that all of the attributes of the universe including mind and matter are different attributes of one God. The word pantheism comes from the Greek words Pan (meaning "all, of everything") and Theos (meaning "god, divine"). Pantheism is closely connected to many famous thinkers including Albert Einstein, Alan Watts, Karl Jung, Friedrich Nietzsche and Carl Sagan. Carl Sagan's son (Dorian Sagan) wrote this about his father's belief:

> *"My father believed in the God of Spinoza and Einstein, God not behind nature, but as nature, equivalent to it."*

There are many monistic philosophies, but some of them are flawed for various reasons. Some monistic theories are flawed because they exclude half of the universe. For example, 'materialist monists', also known as 'physicalists', state that physical matter is the fundamental reality of the universe and so, they conclude that consciousness is merely an abstract derivative of matter (i.e. a by-product of the brain). 'Idealist monists' do the opposite, and they state that matter is a derivative of consciousness. There is also 'Neutral monism' which is flawed because it states that everything is ultimately reducible to one neutral substance, but it doesn't explain how contrasting phenomena such as matter and consciousness come into existence if there is only one neutral substance.

However, some monistic theories don't have these problems and state that the universe is one continuous process whilst incorporating a description of the processes that generate contrasting phenomena. An example of this is the theory of Spinoza's 'dual-aspect monism'. Dual-aspect monism states that matter and consciousness are distinct but are two aspects of the same ultimate, unified, inseparable and irreducible reality. In the last twenty years, within the same tradition as dual-aspect monism, and with the same basic principal, is the theory of 'reflexive monism'. Reflexive monism was created by the psychologist Max Velmans. It states that we (i.e. conscious entities) are not separate from the universe in the way that the tradition of dualism states that we are. Traditional dualism states that mind phenomena are separate from physical phenomena, and so separates our conscious experience from physical matter. In Reflexive monism, the universe is 'psycho-physical', which means that the universe manifests as both physical matter and conscious experience simultaneously and reflexively, and therefore, is ultimately one unified process.

Hindu philosophy contains the non-dualistic/monistic schools of Advaita Vedanta, and the concept of 'Brahman'. Advaita literally translates as 'not two' and Vedanta translates as 'conclusion'. Brahman is defined as the pervasive, genderless, infinite, eternal truth and bliss which does not change, yet is the cause of all changes. In this school of thought Brahman is one with the true self called Atman (i.e. inner self, spirit or soul). Therefore, because Brahman and Atman are one, the underling truth of the universe, according to Advaita Vedanta, is wholeness.

An example in Buddhism is the doctrine of 'dependent arising', which is where all of the phenomena that arise (i.e. comes into existence) in the universe are dependent on the arising of all other phenomena in the universe. That is to say, it's a mutual process, so, for anything to exist it is dependent on the existence of everything else. All things bring each other into existence because all things are one flowing process. This is also similar to the Chinese philosophy of 'yin and yang'. Yin and yang is categorised as a dualistic philosophy because it separates all of the phenomena of the universe into dual opposites such as positive and negative. However, yin and yang can also be used to describe how differences can exist within a monistic philosophy. This is because yin and yang illustrates how all opposites and differences in the universe are inseparable parts of a whole process just like in dependent arising.

Also within Buddhism is the philosophical concept/story of 'Indra's Net'. Indra is a deity who has an infinitely large net which hangs over his palace. At each vertex (i.e. where the cords of the net join) there is a multifaceted jewel, and each jewel reflects every other jewel that exists within the whole infinite net. This metaphor illustrates that the universe is an infinite and inseparable whole at every point within it, because every point of the universe is represented by a jewel containing a reflection of the whole universe within it. This illustrates that nothing in the universe can be separate because everything in the universe contains everything else. Therefore, every point in the universe is as limitless, infinite and vast as the totality of the universe because it is all one.

In physics this reality is expressed in the model of the 'implicate and explicate order' by theoretical quantum physicist David Bohm. In his model, the implicate order or enfolded order is the deeper fundamental reality of wholeness, and the explicate order or unfolded order is the reality of separate fragmented phenomena such as objects, people, thoughts and events. But the explicate order is abstracted from the true reality of implicate wholeness. Bohm says:

> *"The particle is present in the whole and is merely unfolding and manifesting as a separate thing, but it's actual existence is not separate...Everything enfolds into everything and the entire universe is enfolding."*

> *"Quantum process is indivisible. It can be broken but it becomes an entirely different process. Each process is a whole otherwise it can't be what it is. All the quantum processes are linked into one whole"*

In continuous monism, the implicate order is called the 'continuous universe' and the explicate order is called the 'fragmented universe'. The fragmented universe is another key feature of continuous monism. It is the secondary/illusory universe of fragmented parts. In physics, Newtonian laws of motion and causality describe the secondary reality of the fragmented universe (i.e. the explicate order). Therefore, these models of 'secondary' reality, although useful, are inaccurate and are fundamentally a misconstrued interpretation of the universe. The theories of relativity and quantum mechanics attempt to describe the primary reality of the continuous universe. They describe the universe in terms of phenomena that permeate through the whole universe as continuous general fields and waves. These include the wave function of material particles and the fields of gravity, electromagnetism and space-time.

The wave function of material particles is defined as a mathematical probability wave, from which all of the fragmented phenomena of the fragmented world derives. It is the act of direct observation and measurement of the wave of probability that creates the experience of separate parts that make up the fragmented universe. This process is called the 'collapsing of the wave function' within the 'Copenhagen interpretation' of quantum mechanics. The collapsing of the wave function occurs differently, depending on how we measure/observe the universe. That is to say that our observation and measurement collapses the wave function of the wave of probability to create the material world that we can experience as separate objects, such as particles and atoms. We experience ourselves as one of these fragmented objects in space and time. This one wave of probability, from which all of the fragmented substance of the universe emerges, has been discovered within experiments into the nature of atoms within the science of quantum mechanics. In experiments such as the 'double-slit' experiment, it has been discovered that atoms are a wave of probability that is flowing through the whole universe simultaneously, as one undivided process. And, because the universe is made of atoms, it follows that the fundamental reality of the universe is a continuous whole process.

Every atom is a continuous wave until it is measured/observed. Therefore, it is the act of conscious observation that creates the experience of a fragmented separate atom out of a continuous wave. This transformation of the whole wave (i.e. the implicate order or continuous universe) into a separate atom (i.e. the explicate order or the fragmented universe) is the collapsing of the wave function. Here is a quote from an article from LiveScience.com:

"One of the most famous experiments in quantum physics, which first showed how particles can bizarrely behave like waves, has now been carried out on the largest molecules ever.
Researchers have sent molecules containing either 58 or 114 atoms through the so-called double-slit experiment, showing that they cause an interference pattern that can only be explained if the particles act like waves of water, rather than tiny marbles."

Similar to the concept of the mathematical probability wave is the concept of the 'unified field' within the 'unified field theory' in quantum mechanics. The unified field describes the unity at the fundamental level of reality that manifests as the experience of fragmented matter, due to the process of conscious observation. The quantum physicist John Hagelin is a proponent of this theory and here he describes the process of the double-slit experiment:

"an experiment that shows that one electron thrown at a wall which has two holes in it can go through both holes

simultaneously. And those are now called probability waves, that wave that we think of as a particle but it's really not or it couldn't go through both holes. That probability wave goes through both holes and then when the two probabilities emerge on the other side they interact with each other. They interfere with each other. And that shows that an electron is not a thing. It is essentially a concept, a probability wave, and it behaves like a wave. It behaves like math, it doesn't behave like matter."

The question of what constitutes a conscious observer? And, how fundamental is the observer in the process of the universe? are hotly debated questions in quantum physics. A classical physicist or materialist may argue that the conscious observer is not fundamental to the universe, because there was a time before any conscious observers existed in the universe (i.e. just after the big bang), and the universe still existed without the observer. From this, they may conclude that, because consciousness emerged from matter (i.e. the brain), that matter is primary and fundamental, and, therefore, as a result, they may assume that consciousness doesn't really exist as a "concrete" or objective reality. However, this logic is flawed, because there are many fundamental elements of the universe that didn't exist just after the big bang, including electrons. Therefore, using the reasoning of the materialist, we would have to conclude that electrons are not fundamental to the universe. But, if the universe is one flowing process, whatever emerges from the process of the universe is equally as fundamental as any other part of the process because it is all one. To appreciate the flaws in the reasoning of the materialist we can contemplate the process of the growth of anything in the universe. For example, if we think about the growth of a baby in the womb. Simply because a baby's heart grows and develops before its brain, we would not assume that the baby's heart is a more fundamental part of the baby than its brain. The order in which the heart and the brain emerge during the growth of the baby has nothing to tell us about how fundamental they are.

Moreover, there is an experiment called the 'delayed choice experiment' that was created by theoretical physicist John Wheeler. This experiment demonstrates that the act of choosing a particular method of observation and measurement of photons of light, that emanate from distant celestial objects, changes the nature of the whole journey of those photons as they travel through the universe. Therefore, the act of measuring and observing photons has a direct influence on the journey of those photons. And, because the journey of those photons spans a distance of millions of light years, it means that their journey has already taken place millions of years ago. Meaning that our observation of them now, changes their reality in the past. This demonstrates that the conscious observer has an effect on past events in the universe. With regard to this experiment, when describing the fundamental nature of the conscious observer in an interview, the physicist Paul Davis said:

> *"What we do today effects the nature of reality as it was in the past"*

Furthermore, according to many physicists, all points in time flow simultaneously, and so the past and future are concurrent. This means that, not only is the experience of separate fragmented objects in space an illusory interpretation of reality, but the experience of fragmented moments and events in time are also an illusory interpretation of reality.

Meaning, that the past and the future only exist in our imaginations and all events actually take place within the 'infinite present moment'. Events are changes in reality that are all occurring within an infinite now. We only create a past and a future reality in our imaginations in the form of memories and predictions. This reality is explained by Julian Barbour, the theoretical physicist, and author of the book: 'The End of Time'. He states:

"There are things that I would say that you could call an instant of time, or better, a now. As we live we seem to move through a succession of instants of time, nows, and the question is, what are they? They are where everything in the universe is, at this moment, now."

"My ideas about time all developed from the realisation that if nothing were to change we could not say that time passes. Change is primary, time, if it exists at all, is something we deduce from it."

"...each of our instance is part of the totality of everything - is one manifestation of everything"

"The passage of time is simply an illusion created by our brains."

It is also encapsulated by the philosopher Ludwig Wittgenstein when he states:

"If we take eternity to mean not infinite temporal duration but

timelessness, then eternal life belongs to those who live in the present."

Normal everyday conscious perception and the fragmented universe

The enfolded order/the continuous universe unfolds and manifests as the illusion of the unfolded order/the fragmented universe. The fragmented universe is created by the unfolding of the continuous universe within 'Normal everyday conscious perception'. Normal everyday conscious perception is a state of consciousness that is defined by the experience of the fragmented universe. That is to say that when we are experiencing the fragmented universe, then we are looking from the perspective of normal everyday conscious perception. Conscious observation, from this perspective, 'collapses the wave function' of the wave of probability to create the experience of individual atoms and objects out of the primary reality of the continuous universe. When we are experiencing the world from the perspective of normal everyday consciousness then we see all objects, people, thoughts, events etc. as separate fragmented parts. For example, we experience that a cat is separate from a chair. If we then make the assumption that the cat is actually separate from the chair then we are making the incorrect assumption that the fragmented universe is the true reality. In psychology, this is called naive realism - which is the belief that what we experience with our senses is objective reality. Instead, from this perspective, what we experience and call "reality" is actually the interpretation of the totality of flowing phenomena that has been filtered through the senses and presented as a fragmented universe. When we believe that this experience of separate fragmented objects is real then our interpretation of reality is misconstrued and we are deluding ourselves.

The writer and spiritual teacher Eckhart Tolle calls this normal everyday state of perception 'object consciousness'. This is the experience of all of the objects that arise within consciousness, including everything that we experience as sense perceptions, such as objects, our bodies, emotions and thoughts, as the content within consciousness. In an interview in 2020 he said:

> *"Object consciousness, which is all the things that arise in your mind, every thought is an object, a form that arises. every emotion is a form that arises...the content of your life consists of loads of things continuously arising and subsiding. For most people that's all they ever know in their life"*

The philosopher and writer Daniel Dennett encapsulates the delusion of the reality that we experience by comparing our conscious experience with the "user illusion of the screen on a laptop", he states:

> *"You can have a beautiful vision of all that you can do on that user illusion interface but you wouldn't get to the reality of what makes a computer a computer, it would just look like magic. Consciousness is basically the brains user illusion of itself."*

The illusion that Dennett believes he is describing here is the illusion of the conscious mind (i.e. consciousness/awareness itself). However, the illusion that Dennett is actually describing here is the illusion of one mode of consciousness (i.e. 'normal everyday conscious perception' or 'object consciousness'). As a physicalist/materialist Dennett believes that consciousness doesn't really exist, other than as an illusory abstraction that has emerged from the fundamental substance of the universe, that he believes is the materiel substance. Consciousness, he believes, is a by-product of physical processes in the brain and, therefore, has no real existence beyond a description of those physical processes. I propose that this is not true, meaning that, in primary reality, both consciousness and matter are equally real and fundamental, and both are generating each other simultaneously, and are both fundamental components of the universe. It is our normal everyday conscious experience of the fragmented universe that is the illusory interpretation of reality. And that illusion is what is being described in Dennett's 'user illusion' analogy. Both matter and consciousness are primary parts of one process, in the same way that both north and south exist on a magnet as two parts of one whole magnetic field. But believing that north is separate from south, or that only north actually exists would be a delusional belief. The mind creates the brain as an object in awareness, and the brain creates the mind from the physical processes of the universe. And, because the mind and the brain are one with the process of the whole universe, then it follows that consciousness and matter (in this case, the mind and the brain) are bringing each other into existence. They are creating each other in equal measure because they are one process. That is to say that, although our normal everyday conscious perception creates a representation of the processes of reality, in the same way that the screen on a laptop creates a representation of the internal processes of a computer, consciousness itself is just as real and fundamental as physical matter. In the same way that the screen on the laptop is just as real and fundamental as the inner circuitry.

The self

Another illusion which is generated as the continuous universe unfolds into the fragmented universe is the illusion of 'the self'. As a result of experiencing a universe of fragmented parts, we experience ourselves as a separate individual perceiver looking out at the universe, from a specific location in time and space. The self is the experience of ourselves as individuals who seem separate from everything that surrounds us. The philosophy of the self seeks to describe the fundamental features or component parts that go together to create a person's essential being, and the experience of existing as an individual person as an object of its own reflective consciousness. The unique structure of the component parts that go together to create our individual sense of self is called our ego. Daniel Dennett encapsulates the illusory nature of the self by comparing it to an object's centre of gravity in his essay titled: 'The self as a Narrative Centre of Gravity':

> *"This [a centre of gravity] is a well-behaved concept in Newtonian Physics. But a centre of gravity is not an atom or a subatomic particle or any other physical item in the world. It has no mass; it has no colour; it has no physical properties at all, except for spatio-temporal location. It is a fine example of what Hans Reichenbach would call an abstractum...A self is an abstract object, a theorist's fiction"*

In his theory, Dennett states that the self is an abstraction and a convenient fiction just like a character in a novel. Therefore, the component parts that go together to create the self are the same as the elements that a novelist would put together to create a character in the form of words in a book. Similarly, the component parts that go together to create our individual sense of self are in the form of phenomena in our minds that inhabit our conscious awareness.

Eckhart Tolle describes these component parts as the forms that we identify with to create, what he calls, our 'form-identity' (i.e. our sense of being a separate individual self). By using a metaphorical analogy of ourselves as a 'room' within a house, Tolle illustrates how we identify with forms to create our sense of self. during this interview in 2019, he introduces this analogy by roleplaying a conversation with this metaphorical room. He says:

"The room wants to know:
"who am I?".
So, the room would say:
"well, there's this furniture here, there's the sofa and the chairs and the table, and there's the wall and the ceiling and the floor and there's this and that and that's me"
...And then you ask the room:
"Is there anything else that you have missed that you are?".
"No, because I'm looking for more content and that's all the content that I am".
And then suddenly you point out:
"You missed the essence of who you are and that's the space in this room [which] is the essence of the room."
The essence of the room is not the content in the room, it's the

space of this room. That's the essence...In this analogy, that space is the space of consciousness within you. You are not the content of your mind. The content of your mind is your form-identity. That includes all the things that constitute who you are on the level of form. Which is the body, things you interact with, sense perceptions and thoughts."

The content of the room is the fragmented parts of the fragmented universe that we experience from the perspective of normal everyday conscious perception. We identify with those fragments to create a sense of self/ego-identity/form-identity. The experience of being the space of the room, where all of the content arises and subsides in a continuous process, is the experience of being one with the continuous universe. Eckhart Tolle calls the experience of being the space of the room: 'space consciousness'. From the perspective of space consciousness, we experience the process of the space of the room and the forms that exist within the room, which constitute the continuous universe, as our truest essence.

'The bundle theory of self' by David Hume also describes the self as a collection of mind phenomena/perceptions that are in flux, and so within his theory there is no constant and unchanging self. Therefore, the self that we experience is the process of identification with fluctuating perceptions, as Hume said:

"I may venture to affirm of the rest of mankind, that they are nothing but a bundle or collection of different perceptions, which succeed each other with inconceivable rapidity, and are in a perpetual flux and movement"

The bundle theory of self is encapsulated by the thought experiment of 'the ship of Theseus'. For this experiment, we must imagine the ship of Theseus, and imagine, as time passes the ship gets old and its parts decay and deteriorate and, therefore, its parts need to be replaced. Eventually all of the ship's parts get replaced until none of its original component parts remain. Then the question is: does the ship of Theseus exist anymore? And if not then did it ever exist? The answer is that the ship of Theseus does exist but only as an idea in our minds generated by the experience of a collection of fluctuating component parts. There is no constant and unchanging ship outside of our subjective experience. That is to say that all individual fragmented things, like the ship of Theseus, are an illusory interpretation of actual reality. It is the simultaneous flowing and fluctuating moving parts and processes that is the only true reality.

The self is made of component parts in the form of mind phenomena. Therefore, each of us is a fictional character consisting of transient component parts in our brains/imaginations. These component parts flow into a pattern within our imagination to create a sense of self/ego-identity/form-identity. To illustrate this, we can think about all of the changes in our personal opinions and beliefs that we experience throughout our lifetimes. If opinions and beliefs are phenomena that go together to define our sense of self, then there is no consistent individual outside of these fluctuating mind phenomena.

Within continuous monism, the fundamental mind phenomena that go together to create the illusion of the self are broken down into four categories. The first is 'localised temporal perception'. This is the perception that all events in the universe exist along a timeline from the past to the future. Within this timeline there are infinite stories that we can imagine. We imagine our own life story as a series of events along this timeline, constructed from our memories and our future predictions. We experience ourselves at a specific point in time along this timeline from an imaginary past to an imaginary future. Within continuous monism this story is called the 'ego-story' or the 'story-of-the-self'.

The second mind phenomenon is called 'localised spatial perception'. This is the perception of space that is split up into separate fragmented locations. We experience ourself at one of these specific locations in space within the fragmented universe. That is to say that we look at the world through our own eyes from a specific location.

The third mind phenomenon is called 'personal free will'. This is the perception of having control/volition over ourselves (i.e. our mind and body) and the perception of not having control/volition over our environment (i.e. everything that is not our mind or body).

The forth mind phenomenon is called 'secondary language'. This is the language that we use to describe the reality of ourselves in terms of a separate person within the fragmented universe. All of these mind phenomena construct the delusional misconstrued interpretation of ourselves as a separate fragmented part of the universe (i.e. a self).

Spiritually enlightened consciousness

There are many practices, disciplines, rituals and psychedelic substances that can change our experience of reality, from the misconstrued interpretation of reality, presented by normal everyday conscious perception, and into another state of consciousness. These ways of altering our experience of reality have been documented and practiced within positive phycology, spiritual disciplines, shamanic rituals, psychedelic therapies and more. During these different modes of experience, it is possible for normal everyday conscious perception to transform into 'spiritually enlightened conscious perception'. This transformation occurs because of the dissolution of all of the mind phenomena that create the illusory experience of ourselves as a separate individual. This is called 'ego-dissolution' or 'ego-death'. When we experience ego-dissolution then the experience of the individual self dissolves and our awareness expands to encompass much wider aspects of the universe as we become aware of ourselves as a continuation of the process of the universe. Spiritually enlightened conscious perception is defined by the suspension of the perception of ourselves as a separate individual. During spiritually enlighten conscious experiences, all points in time and space flow concurrently in the infinite present moment. Also, our awareness expands beyond our personal free will perception and into, what I call, 'transpersonal free will'. 'Transpersonal free will' is a fundamental feature of consciousness itself. Transpersonal free will dictates the collapse of the wave function of the wave of probability and, therefore, dictates the pattern of all of the mind and material substance of the universe. Transpersonal free will is entangled with the continuous network of all individual conscious minds, in relationship with the random and determined processes of the physical universe. This process manifests as the events that we experience and the behaviours that we display. This continuous relationship between transpersonal free will and the physical world is experienced as one unified and continuous process during experiences of spiritually enlightened conscious perception.

However, spiritually enlightened conscious perception is not a strange, paranormal, magical or supernatural experience. It is the experience of what we actually are. It is the experience of primary reality, and our fundamental essence. Spiritually enlightened conscious perception is called many things within many different philosophies. As mentioned previously, Eckhart Tolle calls this state: 'space consciousness'. In positive psychology, it is called 'flow state' or 'being in the zone'. In Indian Buddhism, it's called 'Bodhi'. In Japanese Buddhism, it's called 'satori'. Richard Maurice Bucke is a psychiatrist and author of the book: 'Cosmic Consciousness: A Study in the Evolution of the Human Mind' and he calls this state 'cosmic consciousness'. Within 'Transcendental Meditation' it is called 'transcendence'. Within the model of 'Spiral Dynamics Integral', written by Don Beck, this state is called 'turquoise consciousness state'. Within the 'Eight-Circuit Model of Consciousness', created by Timothy Leary, it is the eighth circuit of consciousness, called: 'the neuro-atomic metaphysiological circuit' or 'the non-local quantum circuit'. More general terms for this state include: 'mystical consciousness', 'spiritual awakening' and 'spiritual enlightenment'. I will present the evidence that these states of consciousness are all fundamentally the same state but described from within the framework of different conceptual models/theories/maps of reality.

There is a possible problem with the use of the term 'spiritual enlightenment' within the context of continuous monism. Because, it may seem to imply more emphasis on the conscious mind (i.e. the spirit), and not on the physical body (i.e. matter), but this is not the case. Continuous monism focuses on the conscious mind and the physical body in equal measure. I will use the term spiritual enlightenment because it is an established translation of many of the states of consciousness listed above, such as 'Bodhi' within Buddhism, and 'Brahman' within Hinduism.

Recapping the terminology within continuous monism

We have a normal everyday conscious state of perception, which is defined by the illusory experience of the fragmented universe, which consists of separate fragmented parts. We experience one of those fragmented parts as ourselves/the-self, which is what we describe as "myself" or "me", which is distinct from everything else that is described as 'other'. The self is defined by four mind phenomena, which are called: localised temporal perception, localised spatial perception, personal free will perception and secondary language. When a technique such as meditation is practiced then these features can dissolve, which in turn causes ego dissolution, resulting in the experience of spiritually enlightened conscious perception. i.e. The experience of our awareness expanding beyond the boundaries of our individual self/mind and experiencing our true nature as a continuation of the totality of phenomena.

Primary and secondary reality

The universe is experienced and described from two levels of reality. When we experience the universe from a spiritually enlightened perspective then we are experiencing, what I call, 'primary reality'. Primary reality is described using 'primary language'. Primary language describes the continuous universe. When we experience the universe from the perspective of normal everyday consciousness then we are experiencing, what I call, secondary reality, and this is described using 'secondary language'. Secondary language describes the fragmented universe.

For example, if we say: "I am a person in the universe looking at a separate environment", then we are describing secondary reality, using secondary language. But, if we say: "I am the universe looking at itself from the perspective of a subjective illusion, which allows me to pretend that I am not the universe", then I am describing primary reality, using primary language. We describe the universe in terms of secondary reality most of the time. For example, we would usually say the universe "contains things" or is "made up of things", for example, we would say: "there are trillions of planets in space within the universe". However, if we were to describe the universe in terms of primary reality, we would say: "there is nothing that can be described as being "inside" the universe. The planets are not fragmented individual parts of the universe, separated by space. All of the planets and the space flow together as one undivided process. Everything is the continuous universe because it is an unbroken whole."

Definitions for key terminology

Continuous monism – An ontological theory of the universe as a whole uninterrupted process.

The continuous universe – All phenomena (i.e. objects, thoughts, people, events, locations etc.) as an uninterrupted whole process.

The fragmented universe – All phenomena (i.e. objects, thoughts, people, events, locations etc.) as separate fragmented component parts.

Spiritually enlightened conscious perception – The experience of ego dissolution and being continuous with the universe.

Normal everyday conscious perception – The experience of the fragmented universe from the perspective of our individual self.

Primary reality – The experience of being continuous with the universe from the perspective of spiritually enlightened conscious perception.

Primary language – A description of the continuous universe from the perspective of spiritually enlightened conscious perception.

Secondary reality – The experience of the illusory reality of the fragmented universe, from the perspective of our individual self, which is generated within normal everyday conscious perception.

Secondary language – A description of the illusory reality of the fragmented universe, from the perspective of our individual self, which is generated within normal everyday conscious perception.

Localised temporal perception - The sensation of our individual self, i.e. our body and mind, at one location on an imaginary timeline, traveling from the past to the future within the imaginary timeline of the whole universe.

Localised spatial perception – The sensation of our individual self at one specific and fragmented location in space within the universe, which consists of many fragmented locations.

Ego-stories or stories-of-the-self – Stories of our life as an individual within the fragmented universe, from the perspective of our individual self/ego. We identify with ego-stories to create our ego-identity. The story is made of a past and a future that only exists within our imaginations.

Personal free will perception – The sensation of ourselves as a separate autonomous entity, with control/volition over our mind and body, and with no control/volition over anything in our environment.

The-self – The sensation of ourselves as a separate fragmented individual perceiver, within an ego-story, within the fragmented universe. We call the-self "me" or "myself". The-self is constructed by the mind phenomena of localised temporal perception, localised spatial perception, personal free will perception and secondary language.

The ego – The unique structure of the mind phenomena within each individual conscious mind, which make up the-self. The ego creates the sensation of ourselves as a separate fragmented individual perceiver, by differentiating us from all other ego structures, i.e. all other selves.

Ego-identity – The identification of ourselves as a separate individual perceiver, within an ego-story, and with a persona. The ego-stories and personas that we identify with create our ego-identity.

Reality tunnels – Our restricted interpretation of the universe due to our normal everyday conscious perception, which is limited to secondary reality, i.e. the illusory reality of the fragmented universe, from the perspective of the-self.

Ego-dissolution, ego-death, death-of-the-self, or dissolution-of-the-self – The dissolution/death of all of the mind phenomena that create the illusion of the-self. Ego-dissolution results in the experience of spiritually enlightened conscious perception.

The wave of probability or the wave function – The formless, un-manifested and unobservable primary reality of the flow of the totality of phenomena, i.e. the continuous universe, as one wave that splits, i.e. the wave function collapses, to create the experience of the separate phenomena that make up the fragmented universe. These include duel phenomena, such as: observer and observed, subject and object, consciousness and matter. Spiritually enlightened conscious perception is the experience of these fragmented parts as one continuous whole process, i.e. the continuous universe, at the level of primary reality.

Transpersonal free will – A fundamental feature of consciousness, which collapses the wave function of the wave of probability, and, therefore, dictates the pattern of the separate phenomena that make up the experience of the fragmented universe. These include duel phenomena, such as: observer and observed, subject and object, consciousness and matter. Transpersonal free will is entangled in a continuous relationship with the random and determined forces of the physical substance within the universe. This relationship manifests as the events that we experience and the behaviours that we enact. This continuous and entangled relationship, between transpersonal free will and the physical world, is experienced as one unified and continuous process during spiritually enlightened consciousness.

Duality – Dual phenomena, i.e. self and other, mind and matter, north and south etc., which exist in opposition to generate the illusory fragments of the fragmented universe and secondary reality.

Non-duality – The expression that dual phenomena really equate to oneness, i.e. the reality that north and south really equate to one magnetic field.

The infinite present moment – The dissolution of the imagined past and the future, leaving the experience of the present moment as a continuation of the totality of events and phenomena, flowing simultaneously 'now'.

The conscious mind – The element of a person where faculties/mind phenomena, such as sense perceptions, imagination, memories, thoughts, emotions and languages manifest within normal everyday conscious perception. Our mind is where our subjective reality and our sense of self is constructed, by the mind phenomena of localised temporal perception, localised spatial perception, free will perception and secondary language. It is also where these same faculties/mind phenomena can dissolve, which can expand our mind into the unconscious mind and pure awareness, to experience our true essence as a continuation of all phenomena. When the ego structures within the mind dissolve, the boundaries of the mind are no longer confined to the illusion of our individual self. This is spiritually enlightened conscious perception.

Individual conscious awareness – Any internal or external phenomena that is perceived by the individual self, from the perspective of normal everyday conscious perception.

Pure awareness, pure consciousness, the unconscious mind and unconscious awareness –The awareness of any and all phenomena in the universe, regardless of whether or not it is perceived by an individual conscious mind. An example is when we are unconscious and sleeping but will wake up when there is a loud noise, because, although we are not consciously aware of the noise, awareness of the noise within consciousness itself still exists, because, it still wakes us up. Another example is of a baby or young child, who doesn't have a sense of self yet, and, therefore hasn't formed an ego-story or ego-identity yet. Meaning, we can say that a baby has awareness, but does not have individual conscious awareness yet. During spiritually enlightened conscious experience, our awareness expands beyond the illusory boundaries of our individual self, and our individual conscious mind. Our awareness then encompass transpersonal free will, pure consciousness, and primary reality. Therefore, we become aware of what we always are but pretend we are not, which is pure awareness, and the continuous universe, beyond the illusory boundaries of normal everyday conscious perception.

My personal starting point

As I contemplated the world around me, I realised, from a young age, that my experience of reality was not as it seems. For example, in terms of my experience of colours, I realised that I can never know if the colour red that I see is the same colour red that anyone else sees. The colour red, as with all colours, is an illusory experience of a fragmented part, i.e. an isolated wave length, of the continuous flowing wave of the total electromagnetic spectrum. Out of the full wave of the electromagnetic spectrum, normal everyday conscious perception creates the experience of one separate colour, where nothing separate actually exists. Colour vision is a useful way of differentiating the different wavelengths within the total spectrum of light waves, but it doesn't give us the experience of actual reality. It gives us the experience of a useful creation, of an illusory reality, produced by our minds, and projects it out as our subjective reality. The red is created in our imagination as an illusory interpretation of the total flow of the electromagnetic spectrum, and then projected out as a colour that we see in our environment. Therefore, the fact that it's not real means that we're all creating our own red. This becomes even more apparent when we contemplate the perceptual phenomenon that is called synaesthesia. People who have synaesthesia experience sensory input in different cognitive areas of their brain than people without the condition. This means that their sense perceptions overlap. For example, people with the kind of synaesthesia called chromesthesia, experience specific sounds as specific colours simultaneously. For instance, the sound of a creaking door could be experienced as a particular shade of green, therefore demonstrating that colour does not exist within the electromagnetic spectrum. It exists only within our mind. Although I couldn't articulate it in this way when I was a child, this contemplation of colour, and our subjective experience in general, gave me an awareness that the reality that I was perceiving cannot be as it seems.

However, everything that I was learning in school was premised on the assumption that observations and measurements of the physical world can give us an understanding of objective reality. Empirical evidence was taken as truth without questioning the validity of the information that we experience with the senses. And, it's this illusory information from the senses that we are using to construct our model of reality, that we are calling objectively true. Therefore, we're stuck within the limitations of normal everyday conscious perception, constructing an illusory representation of reality, i.e. secondary reality. The truth that we think we find within sensory information/empirical facts are consistencies between our individual illusory interpretations of reality, generated by normal everyday conscious perception. The reason that these consistencies exist is because our normal everyday conscious perception has evolved to generate useful consistencies between our individual illusory interpretations. These consistencies are useful because they allow us to survive and thrive as a species together.

This notion is encapsulated in the 'Interface Theory of Perception', or ITP, that was created by Dr Donald D. Hoffman. ITP is similar to the theory of the 'user illusion' by Daniel Dennett. ITP is the theory that the reality we perceive is a useful construction but is not a true representation of reality. The metaphor he uses is an interface, such as the desktop on our computer, i.e. secondary reality, that allows us to act out processes on the screen but hides the fundamental reality of the computer, i.e. primary reality. He describes it like this:

> *"The language of the interface—pixels and icons—cannot describe the hardware and software it hides. A different language is needed for that: quantum physics, information theory, software languages. The interface helps you craft an email, edit a photo, like a tweet, or copy a file. It hands you the reins of the computer and hides how things actually get done.*

Ignorance of reality can aid command of reality. This claim, out of context, is counterintuitive. But for an interface it's obvious. ITP claims that evolution shaped our senses to be a user interface, tailored to the needs of our species. Our interface hides objective reality and guides adaptive behaviour in our niche. Space-time is our desktop, and physical objects, such as spoons and stars, are icons of the interface of Homo sapiens. Our perceptions of space, time, and objects were shaped by natural selection not to be veridical—not to reveal or reconstruct objective reality—but to let us live long enough to raise offspring."

In an interview in 2019, Hoffman states how the majority of scientists wrongly believe that the evolutionary process of natural selection has selected for the most accurate interpretation of reality. The majority of scientists seem to believe that what we see really exists. Meaning that when we see a cup in front of us then the cup exists as we see it. However, Hoffman says that this is not the case, and he argues that evolution has selected for an interpretation of the universe that gives the greatest 'fitness payoffs'. We have evolved to experience an illusory interpretation of reality that is the most useful, and therefore, effective at keeping us alive long enough to reproduce. Meaning, evolution creates 'tricks' of perception that serve the survival interests of creatures, but these tricks of perception do not match reality. To demonstrate how inaccurate the evolved perceptions of creatures really are, Hoffman uses the example of the Jewel Beetle in Australia.

"This beetle is dimpled and glossy and brown and the females are flightless. The males fly looking for eligible females and when he finds one he alights and mates. But in the outback of Australia there is also another species of homo sapiens, and the males of that species like full beer bottles and they're not interested in empties, and they throw the empties out into the outback. And some of them are dimpled and glossy and just the right shade of brown to catch the fancy of the male jewel beetles, and they were found swarming all over these bottles trying to mate...and unable to figure out that this is not a real female. The species almost went extinct. The males had been successfully mating with females for hundreds of thousands of years. You would think that means that natural selection gave them a true understanding of what a real female is and it's not the case. What evolution apparently gave these beetles was a little trick. A hack. A female is anything dimpled, glossy and brown. So, it's not that we see the truth."

My story

I've always noticed how the story of my life would change depending on the dominant emotion that I was experiencing, at that moment, regardless of my life situation. For example, If the dominant emotion within me was sadness then my life story would become bleak, in those instances I would regret things that I had done in the past, I couldn't imagine anything to hope for in the future and I wouldn't like myself. At those times, my story was a story of a loser and a failure with very little talent or redeeming features in his/my life. Then, at other times, if the dominate emotion was happiness then my life story would become positive, bright, peaceful and optimistic. I would feel good about my past achievements and I would be confident that I could attain my ambitions in the future. I was, in this version of the story, a winner. My story would change from a sad story to a happy story and vice versa. I recognised that these two stories were contrasting and contradictory, so they couldn't both exist simultaneously in an objective reality. It was paradoxical that I could experience both stories and that when I experienced the sad story, it was just as real to me as the happy one. I had inadvertently discovered the illusory nature of my own ego-story. We identify with an imaginary ego-story to have a sense of self. It was this realisation that lead to my fascination and immersion in stories, storytelling and acting.

An actor embodies a fictional character with a fictional story by identifying with the story of the character that is written in the script. Although the character's story is fictional, the actor has to commit to the belief that the story is real, while they are performing the role, in order to feel the emotional consequences of the events in the play. This is the same process of identification with the stories of our own life. We're identifying with a fictional past that we are remembering in our imaginations, just like a past that has been imagined by the writer of the play. The actor is also imagining a future that the character desires, which motivates them to act in a certain way in the play. As an actor, you have to allow this new story to become your own story, in a process which could be described as 'self-hypnosis'. However, we're already 'self-hypnotised' into identifying with our own ego-stories which represent our own lives.

Being an actor lead me to start deconstructing my own character and my own story. I started to question the roles that I am playing in my own life by contemplating questions such as: Why do I want what I want? What story am I imagining that creates the desires that I have? Why do I do the things that I do? How much control do I have over my story? Am I writing my own life like a play? Is there any reason to my life or am I making up the reason as I go along? Is there any real meaning behind my choices or my achievements? Where does my meaning come from?

As well as acting, I also trained as a dancer and as a singer. This is how I had my first experiences of a state of consciousness that was closer to spiritually enlightened conscious perception. I occasionally experienced a heightened state of awareness on stage, or in the rehearsal room, that was often referred to as: 'being lost in the moment'. It was an antidote and the antithesis to all of the stories of my life, and the possible futures, that I had been imagining, striving for and worrying about. I had experienced being 'lost in the moment' on a few occasions but hadn't been able to articulate what this sensation was, or how it was happening. It felt somewhere in between dreams and reality, where my internal impulses would flow freely and instantly materialise in the form of my external physical and vocal expressions. When I was in this state then the words or movements in a performance would manifest effortlessly and spontaneously. I would feel naturally at ease, efficient and relaxed on stage, and none of my actions would seem contrived or strained. The sensitivity of my senses would increase, I would become hyperaware of my body and the bodies of the other performers in the space. The boundaries between us would melt away and the connection between us would become so finely tuned that we could move as one body. My inner monologue, thoughts and sense of self would dissolve or change in an indescribable way, as I would become lost in the performance. I'm calling it a performance but, during this type of experience, the performance becomes irrelevant. There is simply the joy of movement, sound and action for its own sake. However, these experiences were frustratingly ephemeral and elusive. I could experience it during one performance and then during the next performance it could seem impossibly unattainable. I would fight to get it back but the more I tried the more unattainable it became. And so, I became obsessed by this quality of experience during performances or rehearsals. It seemed to be the thing that was worth achieving in my life. I wanted to know what it was and to understand what blocks and barriers prevented me from achieving it. I didn't know at the time that I had been achieving a spiritually enlightened state of perception. The Polish Theatre director Jerzy Grotowski articulates these experiences in his book called Towards a Poor Theatre:

> *"The education of an actor in our theatre is not a matter of teaching him something; we attempt to eliminate his organism's resistance to this psychic process. The result is freedom from the time-lapse between inner impulse and outer reaction in such a way that the impulse is already an outer reaction. Impulse and action are concurrent: the body vanishes, burns, and the spectator sees only a series of visible impulse."*

In terms of continuous monism, the "burning" and "vanishing" of the body that he is describing is the ego-dissolution. The "psychic process" he is referring to is the process of reaching spiritually enlightened conscious perception.

Chapter One: The birth of the self

Atoms with awareness

It is evident that awareness and consciousness are fundamental properties of the universe, based on the fact that we are consciously aware. And because we are a manifestation of the process of the whole universe, this means that the universe is made of conscious awareness as much as it is made of matter. This is to say that the universe is conscious. When we accept the fact that consciousness is a fundamental property of the universe then we can begin to understand how consciousness manifests within conscious individuals, as a subjective experience. In the same way, once we had discovered that the gravitational field is a fundamental property of the universe, we could begin to understand how gravity interacts with objects in space. However, awareness is not confined to the illusory boundaries of our individual conscious minds. Even when phenomena are not perceived by our conscious mind, awareness of phenomena still remains. There are many examples of awareness beyond the conscious perceiver. One example is 'blindsight'. Blindsight is a condition that occurs when the part of a person's brain that contains the faculty for the perception of images, i.e. the visual cortex, is damaged and no longer functions. However, research suggests that although these individuals are completely consciously blind, they are still aware of phenomena in front of their eyes. For example, they will guess the presence of something in their visual field, it's shape, movement, colour and orientation with much more accuracy than if they were guessing based on chance alone. This shows that we are aware of much more than our conscious mind perceives. The question is: How much more phenomena are we aware of that we do not consciously perceive?

Matter and awareness are fundamentally one whole process, as is evident from the fact that we, i.e. consciously aware beings, are both matter, i.e. brains, and awareness, i.e. minds, simultaneously. Therefore, we experience the separation of our mind from matter when no separation actually exists. This is clearly demonstrated within experiments in quantum mechanics. In quantum mechanics, atoms are waves, until they are observed/measured, and then they stop behaving like waves and behave like the smallest fragments of matter within the universe. These fragments include ourselves as the conscious observer and the objects that we perceive as separate from ourselves. This occurs when the conscious observation collapses the wave function of the wave of probability into the pattern of fragmented parts that make up the universe we experience. This pattern of fragmented parts is what we experience as the universe within our normal everyday conscious perception. Awareness and matter flow as one, but this process splits the conscious individual into seemingly separate phenomena from the physical substance of the universe. During this experience, the perspective of the-self becomes the subjective individual, and matter becomes the environment we perceive with normal everyday consciousness.

However, even when we describe the universe from the perspective of a materialist, using the language of classical physics, we will still discover the true nature of the universe and ourselves as oneness. Within classical physics, atoms are the tinniest building blocks of matter that go together to construct all of the physical entities in the universe. Atoms combine in more and more complex configurations to create molecules, chemical compounds and objects with increasing complexity. This process forms the structure of all organic and inorganic entities in the universe. These entities have very different qualities, even though they are all made from the same types of atoms. For example, an entity like a chair is obviously very different from an entity like a person. A chair is inanimate and unconscious, it doesn't think, feel, taste, touch or experience anything. But, those same types of atoms, combine and flow into a different shape and pattern to create sentient beings like you and me. We are conscious and we have an imagination, a sense of self and a sense of autonomy within the universe. We experience a world through our senses. We look out at the world from our own head, out of our own eyes, and we look at an external world around us that seems separate from ourselves. There is a world that we experience from the perspective of ourselves, i.e. our body and mind, and, there is a world outside of ourselves, i.e. our environment, that we exist within. We claim "our" atoms that constitute our body as our own and we call them "me", "I", "my" and "mine". However, they're not our atoms, because the atoms that constitute our bodies are the same types of atoms as the atoms that constitute our environment. Moreover, the atoms within our body and our environment are constantly interchanging as they flow as one process. Researches in the 1950's discovered that 98 percent of our body's atoms are replaced every year.

So, how are the atoms that flow into the shape of our bodies creating the illusion of being separate individual people that are having an experience of themselves as entities that are separate from their environment? How are these atoms creating an experience called "I"? To think about this let's go back to the experience at the start of our lives. Here is a description of the experience of ourselves, coming into existence, from the misconstrued perspective of normal everyday conscious perception:

At some point, towards the beginning of our life, it seems like there is a moment, or a gradual period of time, when our "lights switch on" and we "awaken" and become consciously aware of our environment and ourselves for the first time. However, it seems like we did not awaken from sleep, it felt like we awakened from a void of nothingness. It's like there was nothing, forever, and out of the nothingness came an awareness called "I". Although, if this is the case, it doesn't make sense to say "forever" because time didn't seem to exist for us. Time seems to have begun for us when we started to see, feel, taste and touch. From that moment, we started to experience our specific point of awareness, within a specific timeline, within a world of phenomena outside of ourselves, and separate from ourselves. This is a seemingly obvious observation, that you feel like you and everything else does not feel like you. But this feeling is an illusion because it is not possible for anything to be separate from anything else in the universe because everything, including ourselves, are made of atoms. And all atoms are flowing together in one continuous process to create all phenomena. Here is Einstein using primary language to describe this situation:

> *"A human being is part of the whole called by us the universe...he experiences himself, his thoughts and feelings as something separate from the rest, a kind of optical delusion of his consciousness"*

Here Einstein seems to be saying that the sensation that we have of being separate from our environment is an optical delusion, created by normal everyday conscious perception. For a person to exist they have to grow out of the body of their mother, and she grew out of her mother and so on. They/we all share the same substance. We all grew out of the universe in this undivided process, and so we cannot be separate from the whole process. The process is us. We are continuous with the universe and we are the universe, in the same way that a branch of a tree is the tree because it is continuous with the tree.

We could argue against this notion by saying that a branch of a tree is the tree because it is physically connected to the tree, but we are not physically connected to our environment and so, we could argue that we are separate from our environment. That is to say that there is a physical gap between us and the things around us. Let's think through this problem. What are we? We are our bodies, but more specifically, we are the experience of our bodies in space. We have this experience of ourselves as a separate entity. So, where is this experience of ourselves being generated? If we can locate that place then we can locate where we are and what we are.

We could make a seemingly reasonable assumption that our conscious awareness is created within our brains, so we could say that we are our brain. Using this logic, it would mean that we are separate from our environment because our brain and consciousness is inside our skull and, therefore, everything outside of our skull is separate from us and is not who we are or what we are. However, there is a problem with this logic because it would follow that our other internal organs, like our heart for example, are also separate from us and therefore, our heart must be our environment. Using this reasoning, our heart is the environment of our brain and so our heart is not who we are. But of course, our heart is not separate from us. Our heart is who we are because it is in one continuous process with our brain/nervous system/organism, just like the branch is in a continuous process with the tree. We could say that our heart is only part of who we are. But one part of the process of you is still you because you are continuous with the whole process. Moreover, the brain can't be said to be the localised point where consciousness is created because the brain was created by the process of the universe, as a whole, to begin with. That is to say that our brains grew within the process of nature. Therefore, it is true to say that the process of the whole universe is creating us right now, including our body and our consciousness. Therefore, we can conclude that the-self, as a separate entity, is an illusory interpretation of what we are.

Here is a description of the manifestation of the experience of ourselves within the continuous universe, in terms of physical matter, using primary language:

The atoms that create our nervous system and the-self that we experience as "I", were spread far and wide throughout the universe. They are now, and always have been, flowing into the pattern that is creating our body and nervous system, whilst also continuously flowing back out into the rest of the universe. In addition, our act of conscious perception/observation simultaneously brings these atoms, as fragmented particles, into existence, for us to experience, out of a wave of probability, as is shown in quantum mechanics. The one wave of probability splits into two seemingly separate and duel opposite phenomena, i.e. matter and consciousness, out of what is really only one unified process. Therefore, our sense of self is a product of all phenomena, including consciousness, flowing simultaneously now. However, even when we truly understand ourselves in purely physical terms, we can understand our true nature. That is because we are continuous with everything in our environment, including but not limited to: air, food, water, cosmic rays, the electromagnetic field and trillions of subatomic particles called neutrinos that stream through our bodies all of the time. We have no boundaries. Our environment is what made us when we grew and it continuously flows through us and we are it. To illustrate this, contemplate the fact that we all circulate the same atoms. The carbon atoms that make up our bodies were forged in dying stars millions of years ago. As the astronaut Carl Sagan wrote:

"We are made of star stuff"

He didn't say that our atoms used to be star stuff when they were part of stars. He said that we are literarily star stuff right now because we are made of the same atoms that were forged within stars. Using primary language, we would say that the flowing process of stars and the flowing process of ourselves is one and the same process continuous with all phenomena.

If we look from the perspective of normal everyday conscious perception and see atoms and objects as separate fragments, then we interpret ourselves as merely connected to the universe but not continuous with it. Then we would say something like: "we are separate but physically "connected" to the universe, and so, in that way, we are "part" of a whole universe." This is a mechanical conception of the universe. This would be like saying that we are connected to the universe like a cog is connected to the whole machine. But, we would still be fundamentally separate, because a cog can be replaced by a different cog. However, as the psychologist Alfred Binet states:

> *"The mechanical conception of the universe is nothing but naive realism."*

Or as the author, psychiatrist and literary scholar Iain McGilchrist said when stating that some materialists believe that:

"The world is just a mechanism, it's full of stuff for us to use if we're clever and we are just these play things of chance, robots made by genes that clunk about and then disappear. I don't think this has even a vestige of truth in it. There's nothing in science and nothing in reason that compels us to take this point of view. "

In primary reality, we are continuous with the universe in the same way that a wave is continuous with the whole ocean, because atoms and consciousness are one unified wave of probability, before the process of the universe viewing itself through the human nervous system, splits mind from matter within our normal everyday conscious perception.

It may feel like our skin is a barrier between our body and the world because it protects our organism from the environment, but our skin is really a bridge between ourselves and the environment. There is a constant exchange of electromagnetism, gas, water, atoms, microorganisms and vibrations occurring between us and the environment. We are the oxygen outside our lungs, inside our lungs, in our bloodstream and in every cell in our body.

The way that we describe ourselves using secondary language, is a contributing factor that leads to our belief in the illusion of being separate from our environment. For example, when we express a sentence like: "I have energy, and I use my own energy to lift my arms". When in fact, the energy that we use to lift our arms is created by nuclear fusion within the sun. So, if our energy and the suns energy is the same energy, which it is, that means we are the sun because we share the same energy and therefore we are continuous with the sun. And the suns energy was created in 'the big bang', therefore, there is only one energy in the universe and we all share it. We all are it.

Localised temporal perception

As well as the illusion of the-self being defined by the experience of ourselves as a physical body that is separate from its environment in space (i.e. localised spatial perception), the illusion of the-self is also defined by the experience of ourselves as a separate point of awareness in time that moves along a timeline from the past to the future. This is analogous to one ripple that travels along the surface of a river. The ripple is experienced by an observer at one point along the river at a time but in reality, the ripple is continuous with the whole river and the whole river is flowing as one continuous entity. The past and the future are imaginary and all events and phenomena actually flow as one continuous process within the infinite present moment.

This means that atoms flow through all points in space and time simultaneously, as a wave of probability, until the act of observation/measurement. Then the one wave of the continuous universe interacts with transpersonal free will to split into objects and events that exist at separate locations in space and time within our perception. This means that time, as we experience it, is an illusory interpretation of reality because the past and future are imaginary. When spiritually enlightened conscious perception is achieved then we experience the moment, not as a fragmented fiction but as the whole undivided and entangled flow of events within the infinite present moment.

The self in time

Within the imagined past and future, a story is imagined with a fictional character (i.e. ourselves) in the main role. There are infinite stories for us to imagine. The stories that we identify with are called our ego-stories and those stories create our sense of self and our ego-identity. Our ego-identity differentiates us from all other ego-identities (i.e. selves).

What is the use of the ego-story?

Evolving the ability to imagine the past and predict possible future outcomes, in the form of stories, is an incredibly useful tool that gives us a huge survival advantage as a species. Our stories are also a beautifully creative expression of our unlimited imaginations that are able to envision infinite possibilities for our lives. From the beginning of language, we have passed on stories and knowledge, first by using the spoken word and then by the written word and now by film and computing technology too. This ability to imagine any past and project ourselves into any imagined possible future gives us the capability to plan and manipulate the world for our benefit. This has allowed us to develop technologies and more and more complex human civilisations. However, if we believe that this imagination of ourselves is real then it detaches us from our true nature as an expression of the totality of the flow of phenomena now. While we identify ourselves as an individual in a story then we are identifying with an abstract reality generated within our imaginations. Then we lose the experience of the continuous universe within the infinite present moment. We lose what is real.

Where is the story?

It is precisely this story of being a separate person, detached from the universe, that allows us to believe the delusion that we are actually separate from the universe. It's this illusion of being separate that causes suffering. Our ego-stories are stories of ourselves as a tiny person looking out at a vast universe. If we ask the question: where is our story? Then it becomes clear that the stories are imaginary. If we look around ourselves right now then we can see that our stories don't have any reality in this moment outside our minds. Our story is in the past and the future and, by definition, the past and the future don't exist. The past has gone and the future hasn't happened and can never happen because it's the future. Everything in the universe is manifesting within the infinite present moment called now. Therefore, because all stories consist of the past and future they can only exist as thoughts in our mind within the infinite present moment. We are generating our past and futures in our thoughts and we can prove this in many ways. For example, the School of Psychology in New Zealand published some research with the title:

> *'A picture is worth a thousand lies: using false photographs to create false childhood memories.'*

Through experiments using techniques including suggestion, they successfully implanted false memories into the minds of participants. These included memories as complex as a hot air balloon ride. The subject then identified with the remembered story of the hot air balloon ride and then could recall it even though it never happened. This illustrates that our ego-identity is imaginary because the identity of a person who has been on a hot air balloon ride is different compared to the identity of person who hasn't.

The cycle of suffering: searching for truth in an illusion

> *"If we really saw that it was an illusion, we'd all be happy in our big dream."-Alan Watts (Philosopher)*

Because our ego-stories only exist in our imaginations, the only way to experience anything real is by experiencing our true nature as the continuous universe within the infinite present moment. Everything else is fictional story telling. Therefore, because our stories are not real, we can never be happy if we only try to find happiness within our story because we are searching for something real in an illusion. For example, we all have a desired future which we can imagine and strive for. But the future isn't real and so there is no actual place to get to, although the thoughts about the future are real, they exist only in our imagination. It's the misinterpretation of ourselves as the person within our imaginary ego-story which is preventing our experience of primary reality. As long as we are trying to get to an imagined future then we will never be connected to what is real. This means that we will never get what we want because what we want will always be in a future that never arrives. This creates suffering for ourselves. Pain is the sensation we experience due to damage to our physical body. Whereas, suffering is the sensation that we experience as a result of our past or present reality not matching what we desired or expected our reality to be. We also suffer when we worry that our future reality won't match our expectations either. Suffering manifests as many emotions such as fear, anxiety, regret etc. The belief that our ego-story is real will always create suffering because of the contradiction in the story of trying to find happiness in our imagined future whilst believing that the future, that we are traveling towards, contains our death. Philip Larkin articulates this dread of annihilation in his poem called 'Aubade':

> *"The sure extinction that we travel to*
> *And shall be lost in always. Not to be here,*
> *Not to be anywhere,*
> *And soon; nothing more terrible, nothing more true.*
> *This is a special way of being afraid"*

The illusion of our separate individual self always creates suffering because, in our story, our desires can only manifest in the future and our future also contains our death and the death of everyone that we love. How should we live our lives with the reality of this dilemma in our minds?

The way we live to fulfil future desires is illustrated by some of the titles of best-selling aspirational self-help books including: 'You are a Badass; Start Living an Awesome Life', 'How to Win Friends and Influence People', 'Think and Grow Rich', 'The Science of Getting Rich', 'Awaken the Giant Within', 'The Success Principle' and 'Unlimited Power'. These books can be a very useful tool to plan for our imaginary future as long as we know that the plan is not reality. In the same way that we know that the menu in a restaurant is not the food. However, their popularity is an indicator that we believe that happiness can actually be found in our imaginary future.

When we search for meaning or happiness in the future we suffer in the present moment because in order to desire the future then we have got to define ourselves as unhappy and incomplete right now. By having any desire then we are saying: "I don't want to be me as I am now" and this manifests as discontentment with ourselves at best, and as self-hatred and hatred of the moment (i.e. suffering) at worst. It prevents us from finding happiness, peace or fulfilment in the only thing that actually exists (i.e. the present moment). Or, if we have regrets for what we have done in the past because it hasn't made us happy yet, this too is discontentment or self-hatred (i.e. suffering). This too detaches us from what's real. We create suffering in order to strive for a future we desire. After contemplating this we may think that we should try not to have desires but this is another desire because if we want to live without desires then we are desiring to have no desires. This paradox traps us within our ego-story.

This search for happiness in a future that never arrives is causing our mental health to deteriorate. For example, 85 men kill themselves each week in the United Kingdom and it is the leading cause of death of men under 45. This situation is illustrated by another type of self-help book that focuses on healing ourselves. These books have titles such as: 'Overcoming

Depression', 'Undoing Depression', 'Self Love', 'How to Like Yourself', 'How to Raise Your Self-Esteem' or 'Healing your Emotional Self'. These two types of self-help books (i.e. aspirational and healing) are linked and illustrate our cycle of suffering. The first type of aspirational book illustrates how we believe that our happiness exists in our imagined future and as a consequence, we start to hate ourselves and our life in the present moment. Then, we need to heal all of this suffering which is illustrated by our need for the second type of self-healing self-help book. If we do stop hating ourselves then we can go back to the aspirational books/behaviour and the cycle continues. During an interview in February 2020, the writer and philosopher Alain De Botton talks about the link between these two types of self-help books:

> *"If you live in a culture telling you how to make a million dollars in an afternoon you're going to have a massive self-esteem problem."*

This shows our inability to escape our ego-story and our constant striving to achieve our desires in a non-existent future. The planet also suffers the consequences of this recurrent cycle of human behaviour. The climate emergency, pollution, wildlife and habitat destruction, and the decimation of finite natural resources is a result of our desperation to achieve our goals and attain material wealth before we die.

The self is an alien

We also suffer from our ego-stories because our lives seem to be dictated by luck. Our story is like a movie of our life that we became aware of when our normal everyday conscious perception began early in our lives. We experience being "thrown in" to this movie, "thrown in" to this world, "thrown in" to our own very specific circumstances and we didn't have a choice over any of it. We didn't choose to be born at all, but we were. We didn't choose our parents, our nationality, our house, street, country, climate, family, economic situation, culture, language, the time and date that we were born, diseases that we might have acquired, skin colour, race, how intelligent we are, how attractive we are, our height and on and on it goes.

In our story, it seems like we arrive on earth like a foreigner from nowhere. We have no answers to questions like: why is this my life? What is this all for? Why am I here now and in this place? Is this all just a pointless game of chance? What's my purpose? Why is it so unfair? Why are some people are born into luxury, with a loving family, while others are born into misery, war, disease and poverty? Is it all just blind luck? Then, even if we do manage to live and survive and achieve some "success" in life, we all seem to know how our story ends: All that seems to happen, in the end of our story, from the perspective of our normal everyday conscious experience, we die, and everyone else that we love dies too. It seems like we go back into that void of nothingness, just as it was before we were born. So, if this is true, what's our purpose? What's the point of this fleeting existence? What can we do with our lives to make it worthwhile and to make this time on earth mean something? These questions, although they are useful, they ultimately generate an unresolvable cycle of suffering based on the illusory interpretation of ourselves as a separate alien landing on the planet when we are born. This illusion is generated by the identification with the story of ourselves as an individual who is born, lives along a timeline from the past to the future and then dies. This misconstrued interpretation dissolves when we experience the reality that we are one with the continuous universe. It's the process of normal everyday conscious perception that generates the illusory experience of ourselves, detached from our environment, that creates the story of ourselves as an alien in a foreign world.

The ego-story and ego-identity construction.

Every time we meet someone and ask: "who are you?" the reply that we receive is their ego-story. The reply will be something like: "I am John, I am a writer, I am English, I was born in the UK, I am tall...etc." Take the sentence: "I am a writer". Both the "I" and the "writer" are thoughts in their imagination. These two imaginary abstractions go together to create the fiction of them-self within a story that they identify with as a writer. That creates the imagined fiction of them-self on a timeline. Here is the process: There are infinite stories of writers that we can imagine. We would pick some of those stories and we would identify with some of them. We would also identify with stories of ourselves writing in our past (i.e. memories) and with predictions of ourselves writing in the future and this creates the ego-story/persona: "I am a writer". When we identify with these stories and imagine ourselves in the role/persona of 'the writer' within them, this creates our illusory ego-identity and sense of self.

Now take the sentence "I am tall". We may think that this is simply a fact about who we are but it only exists because we incorporate tallness into our ego-identity. Our height defines us in relation to everyone else but only because we have labelled features of our ego-identity based on height. For example, tallness might denote the self-image of strength, status, power...etc. However, height is arbitrary. We could have based these same features of our ego-identity and self-image on the width of our thumb nails. For example, we could ascribe status or power to people with thin thumb nails. This shows that there is no objective truth to our ego-identity because we are making it up.

Take the story: "I am scared of dogs". There are infinite stories of dogs that can be imagined. Out of those stories of dogs, when we imagine stories of scary dogs and then identify with those scary dog stories we create the ego-story/persona/self-image: "I am scared of dogs". We then imagine a world of scary dogs and we will find evidence to confirm our ego-story which becomes our ego-identity. This world of scary dogs that we have created is our 'reality tunnel' - which is our restricted perception based of our imagined ego-story - and is the bases of our biases, prejudices and beliefs about the world. We can see that our beliefs are an illusion by considering how therapy can change the belief from "I am scared of dogs" to "I am not scared of dogs". A therapist does three things. (1) They try to change the stories that the subject is already imagining and identifying with. These stories may be memories that are often referred to as 'trauma'. (2) They introduce new stories for the subject to imagine and identify with. (3) They introduce the subject to "friendly" dog experiences in their life which they can use as stories to identify with. This proves that there cannot be any objective truth to our ego-identities otherwise it wouldn't be possible to change them.

The only truth that we can say about dogs is that some dogs are scary some of the time. This is the same as saying that all realities/stories exist within an infinite universe. However, we have got to split the infinite continuous universe up into imaginary fragmented phenomena such as scary dogs and then identify with those fragments in order to create our ego-identity and sense of self. This illusion of the-self and our ego-identity differentiates us from each other as separate people.

Every dog that we experience is continuous with the whole universe. To describe a dog completely we would have to include its genetics, current living situation, hunger levels, breed, trauma, sex, and on and on forever until we include all of the information in the universe because a dog is continuous with everything. But it is impossible for us to "know" all of the information in the universe so we create a fiction like: "a scary dog". This ability to manage the total information of the universe by chopping it up into fragmented parts is useful but believing the fiction prevents us from experiencing the true reality of a dog in the infinite present moment.

The writer and philosopher Robert Anton Wilson coined the phrase: 'what-the-thinker-thinks, the-prover-proves'. The 'thinker' is the process of identification with the stories that define our ego-identity. And the prover is the process of editing reality to fit with the story that we identify with. It is like the drop-down menus at the top of our computer screens. If we think: "I'm not a confident person" then this is the role/persona that we will inhabit, like an actor in a play. Therefore, we would click the label that says "unconfident" and a menu would drop down and reveal a list of imagined stories from the past, or possible futures, that justify and generate our lack of confidence. These stories can be hidden from our awareness as they could have been constructed at a preverbal or nonverbal level. The process of "what-the-thinker-thinks-the-prover-proves' creates a feedback loop and a self-fulfilling prophecy for our experiences (i.e. our prejudices) as we edit the world to fit the stories that we identify with (i.e. our reality tunnel).

The more dogmatically we identify with our ego-stories the more hostility we have towards stories which contradict our own. This hostility is required in order to define our own ego-identity because our own ego-identity can only exist in relation to other contrasting ego-identities. Our ego-identities are all creating each other in one continuous flowing process. And it's not just hostility and opposition to others that enforces our ego-identity. They are also defined by the validation of others who share the same ego-identity as we do. We connect to these people by identifying with a group who share particular elements of our ego-identity such as a country, political party, football club, religion etc. The people in the group ratify, endorse and, therefore, strengthen each other's ego-identities.

Here is an example of how our hostility towards others defines us: If we say to a person "your belief is wrong" then they may say "No, my belief is right". That reinforces our identification in our imaginary story. This makes us feel secure in our dogmatic ego-identity and comforted by feeling, even more strongly, that we "know" the "truth" about who we are. Arguing will further entrench the dogmatic identification with an ego-story because we need to be in contrast to others to define ourselves as separate from them. To illustrate this, observe politicians during debates and see how ineffectual these debates are at changing the opinions or beliefs of the people on the opposing sides. The debate only reinforces stories and maintains the oppositional qualities of the two fighting political parties/tribes. Nothing can ever really change as a result of this process because it generates eternal enemies, because we are defining each other with our opposing ego-stories. The longer and harder we argue then the firmer and more extreme our positions become. Until we understand how we are creating the illusion of ourselves then we will never be free from our eternal futile conflict.

Conflict creates conflict: Love is fundamental

Here is an example of two stories within a political context. These are two opposing stories of a man. We can imagine infinite stories of a man but these two opposing stories are based on the same imaginary premise of a man who is (1) living in poverty and (2) receiving financial benefits/government assistance.

Story one: "He's a scrounger and a burden on society. The government shouldn't be giving him handouts. He should get a job and take responsibility for himself like everyone else should. He's not contributing to his fellow citizens or his country. Why should my hard-earned tax money pay for him to live? We should take his benefits and government assistance away because then he will have an incentive to get a job and make money and make a life for himself."

Story two: "Society should take responsibility for its people. He had a below average education and less career opportunities because he grew up in a poor area. The game is rigged, unfair and corrupt with different rules and more opportunities for the rich. If we take his benefits and government assistance away then we take away his basic human rights to food and shelter. That would be cruel and uncaring."

These are two stories that we can identify with as our own ego-story to create our ego-identity. The man in the story is a creation in our imaginations just like the dog in the previous example.

If we were to take any one man living in poverty and expand our understanding of him to include all of the factors and variables that contribute to his life situation then we would find infinite variables. These would include his brain chemistry, family history, the history of the area that he grew up in, his diet, his relationship with his mother, his physical and mental health, his genetics, if he's a minority, how many friends he has and how well educated he is. It would also include the culture where he lives and where that culture originated and developed throughout history. This process would go on and on forever until we would have to included everything in the universe which has brought this man into existence because he is continuous with it all.

People are not abstract political narratives. All people are one and the same as the continuous universe. The argument between which of these two stories/opinions is correct has nothing to do with the man living in poverty because he doesn't exist. It's a process of creating ego-identities that generate a sense of self by using abstract conceptual narratives to differentiate ourselves from one another. Although, we do have to have a process of generating stories to decide how best to organise our society. If we believe that these stories are real then we will never do anything other than create conflict based on illusions. We can only do something real by engaging with actual reality (i.e. primary reality) and not remaining lost in an abstraction (i.e. secondary reality).

If we could experience or accept what we truly are, which is the whole universe experiencing itself subjectively, then there would be nothing for us to be in conflict with because conflict requires illusory ego-identities to be in opposition. Therefore, all that would remain is loving kindness. We would be loving and kind but not because we're defining ourselves as loving and kind. Not because we're identifying with stories of loving kindness but because we're experiencing the primary reality that we are all one with a single universe. Therefore, conflict could no longer exist in the way we experience it now. We would then be free to flow through all opinions, thoughts, emotions and experiences in a dance of infinite potential realities. Then we wouldn't have the need to dogmatically identify with specific fragmented abstract stories to create dogmatic definitions of ourselves. This is not an overly idealistic and convoluted fantasy. It is simply the embodiment of our basic reality.

Other beliefs include: "I think that Mozart is better that Bach", "White people are a superior race", "My country is better than yours", "my religion is the true religion", "my diet is more ethical than yours", "I'm more depressed than you", "I am poorer than you" or "I have a bigger house than you". We can only define ourselves by our differences. This leads to the fear and hate of others who are different because we see them as a threat to our identity because they challenge the stories that we identify with. However, we need to be in conflict with them to continue to define ourselves. But, this doesn't mean that we can ignore these differences either, they must be honoured and acknowledged for what they are. They are the bases of an incredible ability to create an abstract model of reality in our imaginations. This allows us to construct fictional futures that we desire, and this ability gives us a survival advantage as a species. But they are also the source of all of the conflict and suffering in the world. However, they are only a tool made of thoughts. They are not reality. The true reality is oneness, and this oneness comprises all of our differences that flow as one process. Conflict and division manifests within the process of dividing the continuous universe into illusory separate ego-identities within normal everyday conscious perception. Therefore, the ultimate reality of the universe is unity and love because love and unity are primary, whereas our differences are secondary. Love transcends all differences as it is the foundational structure of the universe.

The price of everything

Our ego-identity is defined by stories which have an opposite. This is duality. For example, the ego-identity that is defined by identification with the story "I am scared of dogs" is defined in contrast to identification with the story "I am not scared of dogs". Our ego-identity falls somewhere on the spectrum in between the two extreme opposite positions. Within a capitalist culture, the two defining ego-stories, dictated by having money or not having money are: "I am rich" or "I am poor". Money is an expression of secondary language that we use to describe secondary reality. It's an abstraction. That is to say that money itself is not real. Money is the belief, within our collective imagination, that the worthless sheets of paper, sheets of plastic, metal coins, or numbers in a bank account are actually worth something. This figment of our collective imagination is a useful fiction that enables us to trust complete strangers all over the world, and therefore, trade with them. Trusting each other's belief in the value of money means that we accept money in exchange for things that have actual value. Money is a universal form of exchange that enables us to convert almost everything into almost everything else. For example, apples can be sold and converted into a television, or physical labour can be sold and converted into a holiday. However, we pay a huge price (pun intended) for this useful belief, because, the amount of money we possess also converts into the imagined sense of worth that we ascribe to ourselves and others. That is to say that money is the symbol we use as the basis for our imagined richness or poorness.

For the financial system to define our identities in this way then we all have to identify with the illusory belief that money possesses innate value beyond its material substance. It's a way to structure our imaginary identities. But, believing that money actually has value is the same as believing that a kilometre actually has length. We have created kilometres with our imaginations as a symbol of distance. We know that when we look at a kilometre represented on a map that the map does not contain the distance. However, in a capitalist society we collectively believe that the value represented on the front of a bank note actually denotes its intrinsic value because we use it to define ourselves as rich, successful, famous, admired and talented if we have it. Or as worthless, a loser, destitute, poor or an underachiever if we don't have it. These stories manifest as reality because 'what-the-thinker-thinks, the-prover-proves'. When we identify as rich or poor based on the acquisition of the abstract concept of money then we will prove it to be true in our actions. The majority of the richest individuals in the world live longer healthier lives than poorer people, and have the freedom to travel and live anywhere in the world. They are treated incredibly well, at all times, by most people that they meet. Now compare this to the treatment of the poorest people in society within a wealthy country. We usually step over and ignore the homeless and destitute in the streets and they live much shorter, unhealthier and more undignified lives than richer people. We watch them die in the gutter, suffering from such things as substance addiction and mental health conditions, brought on by the fact that they have no imaginary value (i.e. no money). This is because of our belief in an imaginary hierarchy of individuals based on the amount of money they have acquired. According to a report by Oxfam in 2018: 42 people hold as much wealth as the poorest 3.7 billion. The richest people hoard more money than they could ever possibly spend on themselves. This is because money defines our imaginary value as individuals. Our actual intrinsic value comes from the fact that we are all an equal expression of the continuous universe. Therefore, no one can have more value than anyone else because we are all one and the same. This is what we experience from the perspective of spiritually enlightened conscious perception. However, we have put a price on everyone using the imaginary concept of money to differentiate people into individuals that have worth and those who don't. Oscar Wilde sums this up when he wrote that a cynic is a person who knows...

"The price of everything and the value of nothing."

The Marxist Political Theorist Fredric Jameson said:

"It is easier to imagine the end of the world than an end to capitalism"

This is because we can't imagine who we are without our imaginary ego-identity which is generated by stories/systems like capitalism.

We can see the importance of money in constructing our ego-identities by how the symbols of money physically manifest in the world. For example, we've built gigantic financial empires in every city in every "wealthy" country in the world. These include: huge sky scrapers where we keep track of money and massive shopping malls where we spend it. These buildings stand like colossal cathedrals and monuments to embody and validate our devotion to this imagined system. The historian Yuval Noah Harari wrote the book titled: 'Sapiens: A Brief History of Humankind' where he wrote:

> *"How do you cause people to believe in an imagined order such as Christianity, democracy or capitalism? First, you never admit that the order is imagined."*

And when describing the nature of the self he states:

> *"The self too is an imaginary story, just like nations, gods and money. Each of us has a sophisticated system that throws away most of our experiences, keeps only the few choice samples, mixes them up with bits from movies we saw, novels we read, speeches we heard and from our own day dreams. And weaves, out of all of that jumble, a seemingly coherent story about who I am, where I came from and where I am going. This story tells me what to love, whom to hate and what to do with myself. This story may even cause me to sacrifice my life if that's what the plot requires. We all have our genre. Some people live a tragedy, others inhabit a never ending religious drama, some approach live as if it were an action film, and not a few as if in a comedy. But in the end, they're all just stories."*

The universe experiencing a guy

There is a documentary called 'Jim and Andy: The Great Beyond'. The film documents a time when the actor Jim Carrey played the role of Andy Kaufman for a film called 'Man on the Moon'. For the whole time that the film was being shot Jim Carrey pretended to be Andy Kaufman on set, off set and in his spare time. Jim Carrey had learnt as much detail of Andy Kaufman's life story as he could so that he could accurately depict Kaufman's physicality, belief system, mannerisms and attitudes. He spent time with Andy Kaufman's close friends and family members. The astonishing thing was that they were all acting as if Carrey was Andy Kaufman. Jim Carrey reignited the same arguments with Andy Kaufman's enemies that Kaufman had when he was alive. It was as if the story of Andy Kaufman was being played out again in a new place and time.

Here is the point: it is possible that Jim Carrey was Andy Kaufman during this time. Now we might argue "He's not Andy Kaufman, he's just pretending" but that is the point. We are all pretending to be someone by believing that our identity is defined by a story that doesn't exist. There is no story. Look around you again in this moment, there is no story of you, it's a creation, it's an imagined identity. We are making up our story. Jim Carrey swapped his ego-story and ego-identity with the ego-story and ego-identity of Andy Kaufman which is just the same as being Andy Kaufman.

Although we can't actually experience the world through Jim Carrey's nervous system to know what he was experiencing. That does not affect the conclusion that, in principle, it is not only possible but not actually that unusual, and in this case, it seems that it did happen. That is to say that Jim

Carrey has stated that his sense of self vanished during this time. So, this raises the question: who did he become? I write this from the perspective of an actor who has experienced thoughts that were not "my own" many times during performances.

We may argue against this notion by saying that Jim Carrey can't be Andy Kaufman because Carrey doesn't have Kaufman's memories that he had accumulated over his lifetime, including his trauma, and these memories and traumas dictated his personality. However, Jim Carry can reimagine these traumas and memories, even subconsciously. They may not be accurate or consistent but none of our memories are accurate or consistent throughout our lives, or even from moment to moment. All memories are a process of creative imagination. In fact, our own memories change over time and entire new memories can be implanted in our minds at any moment. The imagined memories that Jim carry creates in order to become Andy Kaufman are just as valid at manifesting Andy Kaufman's inner world as Kaufman's own memories were when he was alive. The point is that none of us can truly, authentically or accurately be ourselves consistently or absolutely over our lives. That's because our sense of self is a fluid and creative process that is influenced by a huge number of factors at any moment and is constantly fluctuating. This means that Jim carry is Andy Kaufman as much as Kaufman was himself when he was alive. The refusal to accept that this is possible is the refusal to let go of our dogmatic ego identity and accept that it is not real in the way it seems to be from the perspective of normal everyday consciousness. Our sense of self is a game that anyone can play if they truly commit to the new identity.

We may also argue that he can't be Andy Kaufman because he is physically a different person with a different set of atoms and DNA. That is true, but Andy Kaufman's identity is an abstract illusion created within the imagination, and so it can be recreated/reimagined. They may not be the same person physically. However, the fact that they have different physical bodies is irrelevant when it comes to the qualities of their sense of self, because their ego-identities are made of the identification with stories.

So, how did Jim Carrey seem to achieve this complete swap of identification from one ego-story to another? The answer is because he was just 'playing', and so he didn't resist the change of ego-identity because when we play our imaginations are not restricted to within the boundaries of our current ego-identity. And because his ego-identity was only a fictitious role/persona in the first place it could switch to another one. We pretend to be who we are. The real truth is that the ego-identity/role of Jim Carrey didn't disappear because it never really existed in the first place, it was just replaced by another game/illusion - another ego-identity labelled as Andy Kaufman.

Our ego-identity is constructed in contrast to all other ego-identities and that is another reason why it is difficult for us to change our role/ego-identity. That is to say that our role exists in relationship to other people and so for example, if we became someone else, our family and friends would say "who are you?". People close to us, such as our mothers, would probably become distressed that we were not ourselves anymore. So, we continue to pretend to be ourselves, not just for the sake of identifying ourselves in relation to others, but for others to identify themselves in relation to us as well. However, Jim Carrey had the opportunity for the people in his life to pretend he was Andy Kaufman too because he had the excuse of being an actor playing a role. And, this in turn had the unexpected consequence of facilitating Jim Carrey's experience of spiritually enlightened conscious perception. He was able to define himself differently because he surrendered the self and accepted this new ego-identity and everyone around him also accepted this new identity. Meaning that his own self of self dissolved.

When it was time to stop filming and it was all over, it was also time for Jim Carrey to go back to being Jim Carrey. It was obvious now to him that he had been pretending to be Jim Carrey his whole life. He could see through the whole game of our identification with fictional stories that we believe are real. Jim Carrey said:

> *"When I heard I had the part, I was looking at the ocean and that's the moment when Andy came back to make his movie... When the movie was over I couldn't remember who I was anymore."*
>
> *"I used to be a guy who's experiencing the world and now I feel like the world and the universe experiencing a guy."*
>
> *"As an actor, you play characters and if you go deep enough into the characters then you realise that your own character's pretty thin to begin with. And then you suddenly have this separation and go: "Who's Jim Carrey? Oh, he doesn't exist actually.""*

He played the character of Andy Kaufman. To put it in primary language: the whole universe was pretending to be Andy Kaufman, in the same way that the whole universe was pretending to be Jim Carrey in the first place. Just like when a musician plays a piano - it's a pattern of the whole universe making a tune. We are choosing to play this particular person that we are pretending to play right now. It's a fluid creative process and in reality, we are not limited to one story, we can be any and all stories because they are made up.

We are not made of these stories because they are merely thought patterns. The philosopher René Descartes, when he was trying to state something fundamentally true about the nature of reality, famously came to the conclusion: “I think therefore I am”. He believed that the only thing he could truly prove is that he thinks and so he believed that his thoughts proved that he exists as an individual. But notice that he is making an assumption about the existence of himself (i.e. the self) as a separate entity who is having the thoughts because he says ‘I’ think therefore ‘I’ am. But he can’t prove that there is a person having the thoughts. As I have shown throughout this chapter, we, as separate individuals, are an illusion made of the identification with imaginary stories, and these stories are also just thoughts. This means the “I” that is experienced as having the thoughts is also constructed out of thoughts. So, he didn’t prove his existence as a separate individual.

All he could reasonably conclude is that thoughts exist and those thoughts give the sensation of being a separate individual self. So, all he could truly state about the nature of reality is: “Thinking is happening” or “There is thinking” but that’s all. The sensation of a separate individual self is an illusion generated by imaginary stories that the whole universe creates in one flowing process. The universe is bringing our life into existence and we are the universe. This maybe be hard to accept from the perspective of our individual selves, as our ego may feel belittled. However, it is not that we don’t exist as individuals. It is that we are actually much more than our individual self because we are also the process of imagination that creates our individual self, within the collective imagination of all individuals.

Chapter Two: Free Will Perception

"A man can do as he wills, but not will as he wills."

- *Arthur Schopenhauer (philosopher)*

Normal everyday conscious perception creates the illusion of the fragmented universe. We experience ourselves as one of those fragments differentiated from all other fragmented parts by our identification with our ego-story that creates a separate ego-identity. Our ego-story is made of the story of ourselves within the story of the rest of the universe. The story of ourselves is like the journey of a character in a novel. One reason that we identify with our particular journey/story is because we feel like we make the decisions for ourselves (i.e. our separate individual mind and body) within the journey. That is to say that our perception of personal free will (i.e. the decisions that we make as an individual) is a key feature that gives us the sensation that our ego-story is our own. Personal free will perception also gives us the sensation of being separate from our environment. We have the sensation of volition over the movements of our body and the thoughts in our mind, and that sensation differentiates us from our environment. Meaning that we have the sensation of control over our bodies and minds and no control over everything else in the universe. Therefore, the sensation that we have of being separate from the universe is based on the sensation of personal free will over ourselves as a separate individual. However, although we experience the sensation of personal free will over ourselves, in actuality, the free will that we experience as a separate autonomous individual is an illusion. This fact is generally accepted within science and philosophy. Here is a quote from the writer and documentarian Raoul Martinez which encapsulates this truth:

> *"There is not a single shred of scientific evidence for the notion of personal freedom. To be responsible for a choice, you have to demonstrate you are responsible for the machinery making that choice. There is simply no way to do that. Nothing in science suggests we are responsible for our cognitive machinery. Once we accept that we do not create ourselves, then our identities, brains, and attitudes, are all not really something for which we can be responsible. They are bestowed to us in the same way that we have brown eyes, or have English as our first language, it's the same with every quality that defines our character or identity."*

Neuroscientist and philosopher Sam Harris writes:

"Free will is an illusion. Our wills are simply not our own making.

Thoughts and intentions emerge from background causes of which we are unaware and over which we exert no conscious control."

"A moment or two of self-scrutiny, and you might observe that you no more decide the next thought you think than the next thought I write"

Here Harris and Martinez believe they are describing the illusion of free will itself, but they are not. What they are actually describing is the illusion of our personal free will perception, as individuals. However, transpersonal free will (i.e. free will itself) does exist. This is the same as describing the illusion of normal everyday conscious perception while accepting the fact that consciousness itself is real. Transpersonal free will exists within an entangled relationship between all individual conscious minds, including our own mind, manifesting as the totality of interrelated thoughts and impulses in relationship with the determined and random forces of physical events and objects in the universe. So, in this sense, we do have free will, but not as separate individuals. Experiences of Transpersonal free will transcend our sense of self, our identities and our individual bodies. Therefore, transpersonal free will encompass much wider aspects of humankind and the universe than the illusory experience of personal free will.

A materialist may argue that there is no free will because the universe is either random or predetermined, just like in any mechanical physical system. However, it has been demonstrated in quantum mechanics that the conscious observer is involved in bringing matter into existence in every moment. For example, in the double slit experiment, the way in which the wave of probability (i.e. the flow of total phenomena), is observed/measured by a conscious observer determines how the wave of probability splits into the pattern of the material substance (i.e. the atoms and particles) that we experience. Therefore, the transpersonal free will within the consciousness of every conscious observer dictates the manifestation of everything in the material universe. If, as a materialist might claim, the universe is dictated purely by predetermined or random physical forces (like a machine), then the universe would be predictable and formulaic but it is not. The fundamental universe, on the quantum level, is probabilistic. The universe is a wave of probability (i.e. a wave of infinite potential realities), until it interacts with transpersonal free will within any conscious observer, and then the nature of this observation dictates how the wave of probability unfolds into the reality that we experience in each moment. When we dissolve our ego, and reach spiritually enlightened conscious perception, then we can access transpersonal free will.

It is our personal free will perception and the sensation of ourselves as a separate autonomous entity that is an illusion. We can test this assertion by analysing the freedom that we have over our own thoughts or movements right now.

For example, if we think of a particular capital city in our minds, we can then ask ourselves: did we have any personal free will over the capital city that we just chose? How or why did we choose that particular city? If we deconstruct our thought process then it becomes obvious that we had no idea how or why we chose it. The process is completely invisible to us. The particular city simply appears in our mind in the same way that a cloud appears in the sky. We have no control over it. We can't possibly know what we are about to think, in the same way that we don't know when the next pimple will arrive on our skin. In the moment that we are set the task of thinking of a capital city then a few capital cities may come into our mind. For example, maybe we thought of Paris, Rome and Manila, and maybe we picked Paris from those three. Maybe we think we picked Paris because we have a personal connection to Paris. That is to say that out of the infinite stories of capital cities that we can imagine, a story of Paris emerged based on our memories. Meaning that we identified with an ego-story of ourselves in Paris. Therefore, our ego-identity gave us the sensation that the choice that we made was ours to make because of our personal connection to Paris. However, this too is not our choice because there are infinite stories of cities that could have appeared in our mind to identify with instead of the story of Paris. Therefore, we are using our ego-identity to give us the belief that the illusory sensation of our own personal free will is real. Moreover, there were lots of capital cities that did not come into our mind. Were we free to choose all of the cities that did not enter into our mind? No, we were not. If we did this process many times then each time would be different. For example, yesterday we may have chosen a different city and tomorrow we may choose a different one and we don't know which city we would choose because the whole process is totally unknowable to our normal everyday conscious mind. An even simpler experiment that reveals our total lack of personal free will over our thoughts is to try and stop having thoughts at all, just for just thirty seconds. And experience that we simply cannot do it. Our physical and mental impulses are all occurring within the process of the whole universe and any sensation of control over those impulses, by ourselves alone, is an illusion that generates the sensation of ourselves as a separate autonomous individual.

However, we can experience the dissolution of this illusion of ourselves as a separate autonomous individual by dissolving our personal free will perception and our ego-identity. This is the process of transforming normal everyday conscious perception into spiritually enlightened conscious perception. This process occurs during meditation when we become the witness of our own thoughts and emotions. That is to say that when we meditate we can watch the manifestation of our thoughts and feelings in the same way that we would observe the sun rising. From within this state of awareness we can become aware of thoughts as they arise in our mind and subside again without the pretence of control over them. During this experience, the sensation of being ourselves dissolves because the sensation of being ourselves is based on the sensation of control over our body and mind, separate from everything else. Therefore, by experiencing that we don't have personal control over our innermost thoughts and feelings then awareness remains without the illusion of the individual self. When we meditate in this way we are experiencing primary reality. This means that we are experiencing our thoughts and actions manifesting without the sensation of our own volition. Therefore, we experience that there is no separate individual having the experience. There is only awareness, and within awareness the self becomes another object manifesting and dissolving out of the wave of probability dictated by transpersonal free will. In the language of Eckhart Tolle, we move from 'object consciousness' into 'space consciousness'. We no longer identify with forms (i.e. our body, things we interact with, sense perceptions and thoughts) and we become the space where all of the forms arise and subside.

On one particular occasion, I was in a park and I was witnessing my thoughts and watching them pass through my mind, and I was also watching a pigeon land on the grass. I was no longer experiencing the sensation of personal free will over my thoughts, so I now experienced this pigeon in a completely different way. During normal everyday conscious experience, I look at pigeons (and all phenomena that exist externally from my mind and body) as being outside of me, separate from me and, therefore, not me. In a fragmented universe, what happens outside of me is out of my control, but during this meditation nothing was under the control of myself as an individual as I witnessed my internal and external world flowing as one. Therefore, the experience of my thoughts was now the same as the experience of seeing the pigeon, because the quality that separated me from the pigeon (i.e. the sensation of separate individual volition) had dissolved. This caused me to laugh because I experienced the primary reality that the pigeon landing in my eye line and thoughts landing in my mind were one unified process which could no longer be defined as me or not as me. There was no individual that I could call me. There was no differentiating quality between the experience of pigeons and the experience of my thoughts. There were no phenomena that I could label as a separate individual me. Therefore, the sensation of being separate from the world around me dissolved. I was witnessing myself (i.e. my internally generated image of myself) in the same way I was witnessing the pigeon. Everything was me and not me simultaneously. It became clear that if I am my thoughts then I am also the pigeons, or if I'm not the pigeons then I am also not my thoughts either. I was not in control of thoughts or pigeons but I was the whole process of pigeons and thoughts. I was not a separate controller of one part of the process, I was simply all of it. I experienced my true essence as the continuous universe when my consciousness extended beyond the illusion of myself and into spiritually enlightened conscious perception. My awareness and free will was no longer confined to the boundaries of my illusory individual self and expanded into the transpersonal interconnected network of phenomena.

Within meditation, this state of non-dualistic consciousness is often called 'Samadhi' which is when we become one with the object that we are observing.

Readiness Potential

It has also been demonstrated through experiments that the personal free will we perceive that we have over our individual physical actions is an illusion. For example, in 1964 physician Hans Helmut Kornhuber conducted an experiment using an EEG machine to measure brain activity. In the experiment, he measured the brain activity of a person when they were choosing to move their finger. The subject would signal the instant that they chose to make the movement, and he discovered that the brain activity, that caused the movement of the finger, had already begun before the person made the decision to move it. They called this pre-brain activity the 'bereitschaftspotential' (BP) or 'readiness potential' as it measures the activity in the motor cortex leading up to a voluntary muscle movement. This means that the scientists know that the subject is going to move before the subject has made the conscious decision to move. In the 1980s Benjamin Libet refined these measurements and measured the duration of the readiness potential to be 0.35 seconds. Meaning that the brain starts the process of the muscle movement 0.35 seconds before the subject's decision to move it. This clearly demonstrates that our personal free will perception is an illusion because the process is taking place before our conscious sensation of volition. The process of movement has already begun and the feeling of volition that we experience is added to our normal everyday conscious awareness after the process that generates the movement has already been established. Therefore, the sensation of our personal free will does not cause our finger to move. The movement of the finger is part of a much larger continuous network of consciousness and physical events that encompass much more than the illusory boundaries of ourselves as individuals. And ultimately, we are one with that entire process at the most essential level of reality. Libet did also discover that the subjects did have the volition to stop the finger from moving at the last moment, even after the readiness potential had already begun. This lead him to come up with the idea that we have 'free won't', which is the power to veto a decision that has already been set in motion. However, if we go back to the previous reasoning based on the 'capital city' thought experiment, then we can reason that a person has no individual control over whether or not they are going to choose to veto the movement from happening or not.

Now think about the physical process of something as simple as speech. When we are talking it feels like we are consciously in control of our speech because we are communicating our own beliefs and opinions. But how can we be in control of the physical act of talking? Let's contemplate the process of our speech: Firstly, an impulse to communicate something appears in our mind which triggers the many positions and movements of our lips, tongue, cheeks, jaw, larynx and so on. Simultaneously, these movements are coordinated with the movements of our diaphragm, lungs and intercostal muscles as our breath is pushed through our vocal cords. The vibrations of our vocal cords are amplified through our body, dictated by the shapes we create with our mouth. This pattern creates the precise pattern of sound waves in the air to manifest as the language we wanted to convey in our original impulse. How are we doing this? We don't consciously know how we are doing it. Our body does it and we have no conscious awareness of how the process is happening. It's too complex for our comprehension. How can we be in control of a process if we have no idea how it is happening? We can't be.

The point is that our internal world and external world is all flowing together as one continuous process. There is no separate individual that controls our internal world and body independently from the whole universe. A way to illustrate what the continuous universe is, and what we are within it, is to imagine a whirlpool on the surface of a river.

The Whirlpool

Imagine a river and imagine that this river is the whole universe. Like all rivers, this river has lots of different features like currents, ripples, waves and meanders. Now imagine that we have walked up to this river at a particular point along the river bank and we see a pattern of a whirlpool on the water's surface. Then we walk away from the river and the next day we return to the same place and we see the same whirlpool because we can recognise its distinctive pattern. Each day we return and we can recognise the same whirlpool. We can give this whirlpool a name. We could call it 'John the whirlpool'. The point is that although it is true to say that John the whirlpool is a separate recognisable feature and is distinguishable from the river as a whole, to say that John the whirlpool is separate from the river would be a total illusion. The whirlpool and the river are one and the same thing. It's true to say that the river is creating John the whirlpool, and it's true to say that John the whirlpool is creating the river. Even the furthest ripples of water and currents that are far away from John the whirlpool are influencing the swirling quality of the water within John the whirlpool. They are one and the same entity. This is exactly analogous to what we are. As individual people, we are whirlpools (i.e. patterns) of energy, consciousness and matter flowing on the surface of one continuous river (i.e. the entire universe). Our atoms were spread throughout the universe, and they are currently flowing into the shape and form that makes up our individual mind and body, as a separate identifiable feature within the whole pattern of atoms and thoughts. The whole universe is flowing into us, through us, and out of us right now without separation. To say that we are separate from the universe is a misconstrued interpretation of reality. We are the whole flow of the universe, but we are labelling a particular pattern within that flow with a name like John or Sarah, and then believing the illusion that John or Sarah exist as separate fragmented individual entities. We are one and the same continuous flow with all atoms and phenomena in space and time, that have ever existed, or will ever exist. We are the whole universe manifesting our own illusory individual normal everyday conscious experience. We are all creating each other as one whole humanity. This is illustrated by thinking about when two whirlpools swirl together in a river. They do not create two different whirlpool patterns. They create one pattern of two whirlpools swirling together. We are the same river.

We may perceive some negative consequences when we contemplate that our personal free will is an illusion. For example, we may think that there would be negative implications if we cannot, for instance, hold an individual personally accountable for their actions. I will argue that the implications of this realisation are actually only positive. There are many reasons why we can’t hold an individual personally accountable for their actions, without taking into account everything that brings an individual's behaviours into existence. Our actions are the result of a network of interconnected physical and psychological processes. These include our DNA, our brain chemistry, the political and philosophical ideologies in our society, the trauma we may have experienced, our cultural traditions, substances that we may have abused or may have been administered to us, our access to education, our access to support, and on and on. Even if we believe that an individual can be born "evil" then this "evil" person is the victim of their own psychological and physiological biology that was bestowed upon them at birth. When we live from the perspective of normal everyday consciousness then our actions manifest as a result of the circumstances of our environment, our psychology and our physiology. This means that, from a normal everyday conscious perspective, we act as a conditioned mechanism because we act out behaviours based on the conditioned patterns that generate our sense of self. However, from a spiritually enlightened conscious perspective, we become liberated from the illusory boundaries and conditioned patterns of our ego-identity. We then become the flow of phenomena, transpersonal free will and pure consciousness that manifests as our behaviour. This makes it possible for us to reimagine ourselves from an infinite number of possible identities and, therefore, we're able to act out any behaviour in response to any circumstances. However, this is not a process of taking control of ourselves, it's a process of letting go of the illusion of ourselves by letting go of the illusion of personal volition. This process expands our awareness to encompass everything that creates our conditioned behaviours, therefore, we become free to manifest any behaviours outside of our previous conditioning. This is the experience of transpersonal free will within pure consciousness (i.e. the creative force of the universe). Ego-dissolution also manifests as love and kindness because love and kindness is fundamental when we experience that the divisions between us are illusory.

Moreover, from a spiritually enlightened perspective, the idea of punishing an individual for their actions is nonsensical. Instead of punishing criminal behaviours it would only make sense to discover and understand the physical, psychological and societal processes that result in the criminal behaviours that we would like to prevent. If someone commits a murder, for example, then we could still incarcerate them to protect the rest of society. However, now we would have compassion and empathy towards that person because we understand that if we swapped places with them then we would have had the same impulse to kill. Meaning that if any of us swapped brains, bodies and life situations with a murderer then we would be the murderer and we would have carried out the same crime because we would be them. This means that incarceration for the purposes of punishment and vengeance will never solve the problem of crime because it will never change the patterns of psychology, physiology and societal structures that cause crimes. Only a spiritually enlightened perspective of love and kindness can bring awareness, understanding and solutions to the phenomena that manifests as criminal behaviour.

Another question that we might ask, when we contemplate that personal free will is an illusion is: "Why should we do anything with our lives? That is to say: why should we continue to play our roles in the world if we don't have the personal freedom to choose what roles we play or how we play them?" When we first gain the understanding that we don't have personal free will over our destiny it can make us feel that our importance and purpose as individuals is diminished, belittled or totally erased. But, when we contemplate the consequences of the fact that our personal free will is an illusion then we actually should feel the opposite way. It doesn't diminish us because, even though it reveals that we, as separate individuals, are not real, we actually have to conclude that we are much more than the illusion of our individual self. That is to say that, although we have no personal free will over ourselves as a small separate organism, we are actually continuous with pure consciousness and transpersonal free will that is manifesting as the totality of phenomena, including ourselves, in every moment. We are the whole universe looking at itself from our particular individual perspectives. Our eyes and the universes eyes are the same eyes. This truth does not belittle what we are. This truth actually expands what we are into something vast and, more importantly, real. Moreover, when we experience that we are not confined to our own dogmatic ego-identity and story, then we become free to experience any story and ego-identity as a flowing creative process with infinite potential. When we experience this (our true essence), then we do have free will, although not personal free will, we are free because we align with transpersonal free will and pure consciousness which exerts a creative force on all of reality. When we experience this, we are aware of reality beyond the restricted view of ourselves as an individual, and so we can truly choose our behaviours because we are no longer a conditioned mechanism. This is not a magical or unattainable state of consciousness, it is our essential reality because we are, actually, not separate from the whole universe.

If this truth makes us feel powerless and small then that is the reaction of our individual sense of self. We are in fact very powerful but not as an individual. At the level of our truest essence we are powerful because we are continuous with the limitless and unbounded power, force and energy of the universe. When we 'let go' of our identification with ourselves as an individual, then we expand ourselves into the true essence of ourselves, which is transpersonal free will and pure consciousness, which is entangled with the physical processes of matter and events in the universe. Then we have actual control over the processes that are manifesting as our behaviours. The story that belittles what we are is the story that we are a tiny organism looking out at a big alien world that is separate from us. This story diminishes us because it's not true so we are believing in a lie. I'm not saying that we don't exist as an individual, I'm saying that we don't exist as an individual separate from all other phenomena. Max Velmans; psychologist and author of the book: 'Consciousness Explained' and creator of the theory of reflexive monism writes:

> *"The process that leads to the thought is still me. So, if I keep going backwards then everything is me because all of the processes in the universe went into creating my thought. I'm immersed in the totality of energetic events. Most of which are below my normal state of awareness."*

> *"We are bits of the universe that experience the rest of the universe we participate in a reflexive process whereby the universe becomes subjectively real to itself. We are participating in the process of the universe trying to realise its own nature."*

Our own nature is that of undivided wholeness, we separate ourselves from our true nature by identifying only with the content of the fragmented universe (i.e. the body, sense perceptions and thoughts). We are actually the process that generates all content as well being one with the content itself.

Extended biology

Every year swallows migrate from the UK to Africa and 44% of them fly to the same nest as the previous year. Then, after a few months they fly back to the UK, also to the same nest, in the same tree that they inhabited during the previous year. Even if they have only been alive for a few weeks they know the way to Africa. When we look at a swallow we see an individual bird that seems separate from its environment. So, how does this creature "know" the way to Africa? Think about how this could be possible. When we believe the illusion that we are separate entities controlling our destiny using our personal free will then this seems impossible to imagine how an individual bird could find its way to another continent ten thousand kilometres away. We have a word for this intrinsic ability for complex behaviour in animals and it's called instinct. However, this word, on its own, is not sufficient to explain exactly what these types of behaviours really imply.

If a swallow is a separate creature, with a separate mind, and personal free will over its actions, that "arrived" on earth when it hatched then it can't possibly have the ability figure out its way to Africa. It only has a tiny brain and doesn't have a rational mind capable of figuring out the journey. For us to travel to Africa it would take time for us to calculate the journey using navigation technologies and maps. And, we would still make mistakes, or take wrong turns but the swallow doesn't take wrong turns. Each swallow simply and effortlessly "knows" the way. These abilities are intrinsic, which means that the swallow "knows" the way to Africa in the same way that we "know" how to breathe. Some kind of map of the planet is encoded into their physiology and ingrained into their collective memory. Every individual bird has a point of conscious awareness. Within that consciousness is the fundamental quality of transpersonal free will which is in a continuous relationship with the determined and random physical processes of matter. The swallow's behaviours are influenced by this continuous dance between both the random and determined processes of matter and the transpersonal free will within consciousness.

The swallows must be continuous with all phenomena to make their journey to Africa. Each individual swallow must be continuous with every swallow that has ever gone before it in order to pass on the information and navigate their way through the landscape. Their awareness extends far beyond their individual mind and body. It may be tempting to find a process which seems to explain how swallows find Africa and then think we understand how they do it, dismissing the true conclusion. For example, we could explain it by saying: "They are navigating their way around the earth by using signals that they receive from the electromagnetic field generated by the earth. They can sense these signals and we can't, so, it seems astonishing to us but it's not." In some ways, this is true: however, it doesn't affect the conclusion that they are continuous with the earth because the electromagnetic field is also continuous with the earth. It's the same as saying that a whirlpool uses the water from the rest of the river to create its pattern. We can see how the awareness of animals extends far beyond the illusion of the separate individual by observing the astonishing spectacle of the murmuration of starlings at dusk. We can observe hundreds of thousands of these birds perfectly and exquisitely in synch with each other as they fly at incredible speeds, through extraordinarily complex formations. We can witness their collective awareness and transpersonal free will in a continuous relationship with the currents of winds that are flowing through the atmosphere.

The idea of the organism being continuous with the whole universe is illustrated by the idea of the extended phenotype created by Richard Dawkins. The extended phenotype describes the effects that an organism's genes have on its environment. It shows that an animal's biology is not confined to its own body. It illustrates how an organism's biological processes are in a continuous relationship with its environment without boundaries. Here is Richard Dawkins from an interview in 2019 describing the process of the extended phenotype in terms of a bird's ability to build a nest.

> *"The extended phenotype is the phenotype which is outside the body in which the gene sits. And, my classic example of this are animal artefacts like bird's nests...The genes are producing that. They're still doing it via embryology but the embryology...reaches outside the body in the form of behaviour. In this case, nest building behaviour. But that's only yet one more step in the embryonic chain of causation. The embryonic chain of causation begins with DNA influencing proteins and that influences something else which influences something else: cell division, neurone production in the brain, which has the eventual consequence of causing the bird to build a nest of a particular shape. So, there's just this chain of causation starting with DNA protein and going through various complicated steps in embryology and then the final steps are outside the body."*

It's the bird's specific genes that build the nest and it's the conditions of the environment that created the necessity for those particular genes to be selected for in the first place. The bird and the environment are one and the same process. It seems counterintuitive to us that our own biology is as much our environment as it is our body, but we are continuous with everything inside and outside of the imaginary boundaries of our organism. For example, the complex journey of one blood cell travelling around our circulatory system is comparable in complexity to the journey that the swallow takes to Africa. However, we don't see the blood cell as a separate entity making its way around the circulatory system of its own volition. We understand that the blood cell is continuous with the process of the whole human organism. But a blood cell in a body is exactly analogous to a swallow in the universe. The universe is like one whole continuous organism. Swallows find Africa in the same way that an oxygenated blood cell finds an organ. The process that gives a swallow the ability to navigate the earth is the same process that gives us the ability to breath, to think, to feel, for oceans to wave, hearts to beat, flames to burn and bees to buzz because there is only one process. Asking "how do they find Africa?" is the same as asking how does rain find the ground? How does sperm find the egg? How does light find my eyes? How do I find someone to love me? How do I learn the English language? How do I choose my next meal? How do the planets spin? How do my toe nails grow? Or how do I live a good life? Because it's all one continuous process of the dance between the random and determined processes of matter and transpersonal free will within consciousness that generates all of the behaviours of the universe.

Where is intelligence?

One of the ways in which we separate ourselves from our true nature is by using secondary language to describe ourselves. For example, we differentiate ourselves from nature by describing our human intelligence as a type of intelligence that doesn't exist in the rest of the natural world (as far as we know). For evidence of our different type of intelligence we refer to our creations and inventions within the realm of science and technology such as computers, aeroplanes, telephones and cars. We say that these devices and tools differentiate us from nature because these things are "man-made", they are not naturally occurring. We say that no other creature in nature has the ability to make such complex objects, so our intelligence is unique and this makes us superior to nature. We also know that the most complex thing in the universe is the human brain so we say the reason that we are so intelligent is because of our big brains. Therefore, it is our big brains that differentiate us from the rest of nature.

However, this belief is created by the identification of ourselves as a separate individual based on a misconstrued interpretation of the universe as a fragmented machine. To prove this, we don't have to think for long before we come to the realisation that we didn't create our brain. Our brain is a naturally occurring organ. Our brains grew from the universe just like a tree. Therefore, by citing our brain as the feature which sets us apart from nature is another example of a way in which we try to separate ourselves from what we truly are. Our intelligence and nature's intelligence is the same intelligence because there is only one form of intelligence. The same intelligence that guides the swallows to Africa also builds computers. We keep looking for separation between us and the world around us to justify our feeling of separation from our environment but no separation exists.

When we compare how a person achieves something to how a plant or an animal achieves the same thing we discover this universal intelligence. For example, think about how we may build a sail boat and use our own intelligence to construct a sail that harnesses the wind to propel the boat along the water. Then ask the questions: is the wind pushing the boat? Or is our intelligence pushing the boat? It's both, because it's one process. Now let's compare this to when a dandelion makes a tiny umbrella for each of its seeds to be carried on the wind. Is the wind carrying the seed? Or is the intelligence of nature carrying the seed? Again, it's both because it's one process. But we wrongly describe a dandelion as unintelligent because we think that we, as an individual, choose to make a sail boat but a dandelion doesn't choose to disperse its seeds on the wind. But really, it's the sensation of personal free will that is the illusion and this illusion causes us to wrongly interpret our intelligence as separate from the intelligence of the universe. Our brains/nervous systems/minds are a point where transpersonal free will manifests within the collective continuous network of all other brains/minds, and in a continuous relationship with all phenomena including dandelions. Intelligence manifests as complex behaviours such as: a swallow flying to Africa, a dandelion dispersing its seeds on the wind, or a man constructing a sail boat. This intelligence is a result of collective learning which is generated by the network of conscious creatures enacting transpersonal free will in a relationship with the random and determined processes of matter (i.e. physical processes such as evolution through natural selection). We experience the random and determined forces of natural selection and the deliberate conscious decisions of our transpersonal free will as opposite and separate phenomena but it is the dance between them, as one uninterrupted process, that generates the totality of events in the universe.

Fragments of a bumble bee

To make any measurement of the universe we have to isolate a bit of the universe to look at it and label it. We view every fragment as if it is a separate whole thing but it can never be a separate fragment outside of the one totality of all phenomena. We can only pretend that it is separate for the purposes of measuring it.

A way to demonstrate this is by measuring something and realising that we can't describe it without also including the description of everything else in the universe. For example, let's say that we are scientists studying a bee's wing. We can't measure it separately from the body of the bee because the wing tells us as much about the bee's body as it does about itself and the bee's body tells us about the bee's wing. This is because they are connected, continuous and in an inseparable relationship with one another. Any feature that we measure which describes the wing only exists because of the features of the body, and vice versa. Then, when we study the bee as a whole individual we learn as much about the environment in which the bee lives because it is continuous with its environment. Then when we study the "separate" environment around the bee we learn about the wider environment including the whole country and its climate conditions, seasons and atmosphere which then tells us about the planet as a whole. Then the planet tells us about the solar system and on and on and on until we are studying the whole universe. But our minds can't study everything at once because we aren't capable of "knowing" all of the information from the entire universe at once. So, we have to study it in tiny little bits but we pretend that these fragmented bits are separate whole things. The world of separate fragmented parts is the secondary reality and a delusion of our normal everyday consciousness.

The synthetic bubble

The illusion of our normal everyday conscious perception physically expresses itself in the way that we organise the world. Our food sits in supermarkets disconnected from the process of how it arrived there. We see each vegetable, grain, meat product and spice wrapped up and labelled in the unchanging and artificial environment of the shop. Experiencing our food like this gives us the sensation of a fragmented universe and detaches us from the whole process of continual growth and decay of all organic matter. The fragmented final product is the only thing that we see. In reality, we are a continuous cycle of all of the nutrients, cells, chemicals and atoms that make up every organism on the planet but we've created a world that gives us the illusion that we're not. For example, by only seeing a chicken wing, separate and wrapped up in plastic instead of seeing the chicken's entire life cycle we see the fiction of a fragmented representation of reality.

This idea can be extrapolated to include the illusion of artificiality of our towns and cities. I say 'illusion' of artificiality because nothing is actually artificial but we have created a world where we only experience a contrived and superficial interpretation of the things around us. For example, we experience chalk as a tool that enables us to write on a black board. But chalk has been formed over the last ninety million years as the shells of billions of microorganisms called 'Coccolithophres' accumulate and compress deep underneath the ocean. Chalk is continuous with the complex history of the biological and geological processes of the planet. Our cities don't express these deeper truths and instead keep us in a phoney bubble where the universe is reduced to a meaningless, synthetic and manufactured presentation of reality.

Chapter Three: Localised spatial Perception

"As observers, we are personally involved with the creation of our own reality. Physicists are being forced to admit that the universe is a mental construction." - R. C. Henry (Physicist and Astronomer)

"The universe is beginning to look more like a great thought than like a great machine. Mind no long appears to be an accidental intruder into the realm of matter, we ought rather [to] hail it as the creator and governor of the realm of matter." - Sir James Jeans (Physicist)

"Reality gets created through acts of observation." "Consciousness is the creative element of the universe, without

it nothing would appear." - Fred Alan Wolf (Theoretical Physicist)

Localised spatial perception is the sensation of ourselves (i.e. our body and mind) at one specific and fragmented location in space within the universe which consists of many fragmented locations. It's the specific place in space from where our normal everyday conscious experience is located (i.e. the place from where our eyes look out at the world around us). This experience consists of the illusion of two fragmented realities or worlds. One world is the "inside" world which is made of mind phenomena and the other world is the "outside" world made of physical matter which is "outside" our mind. A good way to illustrate how this interpretation of our experience is false is to consider an object that we perceive in front of us, like a cup, and ask the question: "How do we experience this object as separate from ourselves?"

The cup inside and outside the mind

Consider the process of perceiving/seeing/experiencing a cup. I am going to break this down in terms of our sense of sight because it is our primary sense but the principal is the same for all of our senses. Firstly, light shines on the cup and bounces off it, then that light lands on our eyes. Our eyes detect the light and turn those patterns of light waves into electrical impulses which travel along our optic nerve to our brain. Our brain translates those impulses to create an image/experience of the cup. All of these images and sensations in our brain constitute our conscious mind. So, our brain creates our mind and then our mind is projected "out" as the representation of our environment, which includes the image of the cup that we experience as being outside of ourselves. This means that there are two cups. There is the cup that we have created in our mind from the electrical impulses that our brain received and there is the original cup that is "out there" and was hit by the light that we received on our retina. We can't actually experience the original cup directly because we can't have direct contact with that original cup. We only have indirect contact with it via the light that bounced off it and hit our eyes. Our brains then translate that pattern of light into the visual cup we experience but that experience was created in our mind. Therefore, we can conclude that there seems to be two cups - a cup in our mind and a cup "out there" in the world. This is duality. The world is split into two - the internal and the external or the self and the other or the observer and the observed or the mind and the matter. This is known as the mind-body problem, which is the problem of there being two separate worlds of existence. One world consists of consciousness and the other consists of physical matter. However, we can see that there is a close relationship between the external cup and the internal cup because the internal cup is created using the light that bounced off the external cup. That is to say that there is a transaction going on between the two worlds.

We can see this relationship clearly if we imagine pain. Imagine that we have a pain in our finger. The pain is perceived "out there" in our finger but we know that pain is only generated by the mind as an interpretation of damage to the finger. But we can take a physical drug that kills pain and the physical pill changes our physical brain chemistry and the pain goes away. Therefore, we can see a clear transactional relationship between the physical world, i.e. the pill and the world in our mind, i.e. the pain.

Next, we will deconstruct our experience of the cup again. But this time we will explore exactly how fundamentally intertwined the relationship is between ourselves, i.e. 'the observer', and the cup, i.e. 'the observed'. On the physical side of the relationship there is a physical cup, physical light, physical eyes, a physical nervous system and a physical brain. Then the brain creates the other side of the relationship which is the mind and the mind creates the cup that we experience. We experience a projected three-dimensional cup outside of our head but it only actually exists in our mind. Here's the key detail: We experience the cup as an object in space and our head is also an object in space that we experience in the same way. If we were to chop open our skull we would see our brain and we would experience our brain as an object in space in exactly the same way that we experience the cup. This has important implications. This means that the cup is created in our mind and our mind is created in our brain. Which means that our brain creates our mind and our mind then creates the brain that we experience as an object in space just like the cup. So, our brain creates our mind and our mind creates our brain. Now we have gone as deep as we possibly can into the process of experience and we can see that separation is impossible. There is only one indivisible process. Mind and matter cannot be separated because they are creating each other and they need each other to exist at all. The brain is matter and it creates the mind. The mind is consciousness and it creates the brain as the matter that we experience. Mind creates matter and matter creates mind. When we get deep enough into reality and the process of duality then we see that both sides of mind and matter enfold into one process and unfold to create the illusion of two separate phenomena. The brain is simultaneously generating consciousness and creating itself as an object within the consciousness that it creates. This may seem like a convoluted, counterintuitive or strange notion at first, but once we explore many other examples of how the reality of duality unfolds it becomes a simple and obvious notion.

We could argue against this notion by saying that we can measure the cup objectively and separately from ourselves by using external measuring devices like a video recorder to "see" the cup. However, this argument doesn't work because those measuring devices are in the same place as the cup. So, we can use the same thought process that we have used above to realise that we are not separate from any measuring devices that we use to make any measurement. As the writer and philosopher Robert Anton Wilson says:

> *"Any reading of the universe is inaccurate if you don't include the machine that you use to take your reading and if the only machine that we have to make a reading is the human nervous system then you have to include the human nervous system in your reading".*

He also talks about the first question in Zen Buddhism being:

> *"Who is the master who makes the grass green? The word Yoga means yolk or union...The greenness of the grass is a transaction between you and the grass...It's a coincidence of contraries between the grass and the human nervous system which creates the greenness of the grass...You're experiencing your union with everything all of the time otherwise you wouldn't be experiencing anything"*

Duality and more stories

To reiterate: mind and matter seem separate in a dualistic universe but are in fact one process because each pair of opposites are actually one and the same. This process is depicted in the doctrine of dependent arising in Buddhism and is also echoed in the Chinese philosophy of Yin and Yang. Everything in the universe has an opposite and requires its opposite in order for it to exist. Day can't exist without night, up creates down, black creates white, sad needs happy, self and other are one and the same on a spectrum of opposites. Consider the opposites of north and south for example. One whole magnet requires the north pole and the south pole for the whole magnet to exist. We can't remove north and keep a magnet. Both north and south are required to enable the existence of the whole magnet because they create each other. We experience north as separate from south but this is an illusion. In the same way: the cup is us and we are the cup because we are bringing each other into existence by being opposites as observer and observed or subject and object. Our separation from the cup is a false perception. Our false perception of reality is encapsulated in the clichéd and seemingly paradoxical question: "What came first, the chicken or the egg?". All chickens and all eggs are one simultaneous process which cannot be separated but we wrongly experience eggs as separate from chickens which is impossible.

This is why, within many spiritual teachings you often hear seemingly clichéd phrases such as: "We are all one" or "Everything is one". I understand how a sceptical person could logically conclude that this is not true because by stating that we are all one it seems to suggest that we are all one amorphous blob of the same indistinguishable stuff. We could argue: "We're not all one. How can we be one and the same if we are all different?". However, this logic has misinterpreted what is really meant by oneness. We are all one but not because we are all the same. We are all one because of our differences. We are all one within a system of opposites. It's our differences that define us as the same on the spectrum of opposites that are all creating each other. For example: our opinions and beliefs are elements that differentiate us as separate individuals from other people who have the opposite opinions and beliefs. My opinions and beliefs can only exist if there are others who have the opposite opinions and beliefs to mine. If all of the people with the opposite opinions and beliefs to me die or disappear then that part of me dies and disappears. If my differentiating qualities disappear then so does my ego-identity. Those opinions and beliefs can only exist in opposition to the opposite opinions and beliefs because they are really the same on a spectrum like north and south on a magnet or like the front and back of one object.

For example: an argument has two sides. One side says "I'm right and you're wrong" and the other side says "I'm right and you're wrong". Each side thinks they are trying to change the opinion of the person on the other side of the argument but that is an illusion. In fact, they are creating the identity of their opponent and they are creating their own identity in opposition to their opponents. Therefore, the more we argue with each other the more we will polarise our identities and move to a more and more extreme position on the spectrum of opposites. All augments or discussions that are devoid of a spiritually enlightened perspective will lead to the creation of more extreme dogmatic ideological individual and tribal identities and, therefore, more conflict.

A good way to illustrate how we are all creating our identities together as one flowing process of collective/transpersonal free will is to imagine a

Ouija board. A group of participants stand around a board with letters on it. They all place their hands on a small piece of wood called a planchette. Somebody then asks a question and then the planchette moves across the Ouija board, stopping on each letter to write a reply. However, none of the individual participants are consciously controlling the planchette's movements. From the perspective of the individual participants, the planchette is writing of its own volition. The group is writing the answer in unison but with no sensation of their own personal control over the process as individuals. Their sensation of being autonomous individuals has been removed because the writing is simply happening and they are witnessing it. The Ouija board is a brilliantly simple way to clearly demonstrate that personal free will is an illusion and to experience the truth of transpersonal free will. The so called "separate" minds of the participants act as one, without planning their movements, they become perfectly coordinated and synchronized as their hands move together to write the answer. In 1852 a British physiologist called William Benjamin Carpenter introduced a theory called Ideomotor action. The theory was put into the mainstream by the physician William James in his 1890 book called Principles of Psychology. The theory states that not all of the actions of our muscles arise because we deliberately and consciously make them occur of our own free will. These actions can be hidden from our conscious awareness altogether and there is some other driving force underneath our conscious attention that is moving our muscles. It states that our subconscious expectations for a particular outcome causes the movement to occur in this desired way, hidden from our conscious mind. As the previous example of the bereitshaftspotential/readiness potential clearly demonstrates, all movement is really occurring outside of our conscious awareness but our sensation of personal free will is added to give us a sense of individual control. The Ouija board demonstrates the true nature of all actions and decisions of human beings as flowing together in an entangled network of transpersonal free will.

We can see this reality being played out on social media sites such as Facebook. Our individual stories on Facebook are being co-written by everyone else on Facebook, and by the Facebook algorithm. All Facebook profiles are writing each other in the same way that all of the participants playing with a Ouija board are moving the planchette to write something together. However, instead of a group of people being connected by their fingers via a planchette connected to letters on a Ouija board, the fingers of the participants on Facebook are connected to letters on a keyboard which are connected to the internet. To return to the metaphor of each individual being a whirlpool in a river. We can imagine lots of individuals represented by lots of whirlpools and we can see that all of the whirlpools flow through each other and create each other as one whole flowing totality of water. In the same way, we are all one entity of opinions and beliefs all swirling as one pattern of information that flows together writing all our stories simultaneously.

Facebook takes advantage of our illusion of personal individual autonomy by using algorithms to measure and analyse the total flow of information to predict and manipulate our individual behaviours. They can do this because, while we are acting from the illusory perspective of our separate self then we are trapped within the established behavioural patterns of our ego-identity. The total flow of digital information contains the pattern of our ego-stories flowing as one because it contains our desires and regrets, our passions and frustrations etc. Therefore, the algorithm can artificially increase our desires or create new desires within us as they choose. This means that our belief that we are individuals with personal free will, separate from the totality of information, allows us to be manipulated by an algorithm. It is only by reaching a spiritually enlightened perspective that will give us an understanding of how our own behaviours manifest as one flowing collective of conscious minds. This understanding will make us able to defend ourselves against this type of manipulation. A spiritually enlightened perspective will allow us to make decisions that aren't dictated by the ridged pattern of our established ego-identities. That is to say that, from a spiritually enlightened perspective, our identity becomes a creative process with infinite possibilities, unrestricted by the illusion of ourselves as an individual.

These algorithms can predict our behaviours as long as we remain within the boundaries of our dogmatic ego-identities. Therefore, the algorithms manipulate us by keeping us arguing and in perpetual conflict with one another. The more we argue the more clearly defined our ego-identities become and we polarise to the extreme ends of the spectrums of opinions and beliefs. The more unequivocally we act out the current patterns of our ego-identities, based on our social and biological conditioning, the more predictable and easily influenced we become and the longer the social media site can hold our attention. So, Facebook's algorithms will generate as much hostility, anger, hatred, resentment and tribalism as possible to predict and manipulate us for profit. This was encapsulated in 2019 in an exchange between the neuroscientist and writer Sam Harris, and the business man and writer of the book: 'Zucked: Waking Up to the Facebook Catastrophe' Roger McNamee:

> *Sam Harris - "Misinformation spreads more effectively than facts. The more lurid story is more clickable than the more nuanced one, and you add to that the emotional component:*

that outrage increases peoples time on any social media site. And this leads to an amplification of tribalism and partisanship and conspiracy theory. All of these things are more profitable than a healthy conversation about facts...given the business model."

Roger McNamee - "When I think about the problem, that's one piece of it - which is the manipulation of people's attention for profit and the natural divisiveness of using fear and outrage and filter bubbles that isolate people... if you start out anti-vaccination curious and they can get you into an anti-vacs group, within a year you're going to be in the streets fighting vaccination. It's just how it works. That constant reinforcement makes your position more rigid and makes them more extreme and we cannot help that...it's not a question of character or whatever, it's about the most basic evolutionary wiring."

When talking about the manipulation of our attention by social media for profit, Shoshana Zuboff - author of 'The Age of Surveillance Capitalism' said this:

"It's a marketplace that trades exclusively in human futures."

Social media amplifies the illusion of our ego-identity as the primary reality. This is because we each create a map of our ego-stories by picking out and isolating fragmented parts of our past in the form of photographs and opinions that we identify with and therefore, want to represent us. We place these fragments in an order on a timeline to construct a story of our lives. We consciously edit and curate images and descriptions of our lives to manufacture a fictional persona to display to the world. We have many personas/ego-stories that we present at different times or in different situations in our lives. Whichever ego-story we identify with at any moment creates the illusion of ourselves at that time. The fact that we identify with many ego-stories and the fact that we can change our identification at any time is clear evidence that our ego-identities are an illusion.

When somebody visits our home, they knock on the door and we shout “Who is it?”. The reply we receive then dictates how we edit our identity. We then identify with the particular ego-story which fits with our relationship to that particular person. If it’s our mother then we adopt a different ego-identity than if it were a stranger or our best friend. For example, our mother might say: “You always take too long to answer the door”. This is a story of her son or daughter that she is creating and identifying with to have a sense of herself in relationship to an imagined identity of her son or daughter. Then, we will agree or disagree with her story to create our own imagined ego-identity. Our relationship to the person at the door dictates who we are. However, it’s not just other people that dictate the illusion. All people and events dictate who we are in a continuous universe.

On social media, the illusion of our separate self is set in the virtual world seemingly for eternity. Our Facebook page can reinforce our identification with our ego-story by projecting it onto a screen to make it seem real and tangible. This projected version of our virtual self is then reinforced further by the act of validation, affirmation or refutation by other Facebook users who endorse, ratify or rebut our ego-identity by liking or disliking our opinions and images.

The Big Bang

As scientists have looked as deeply as they can into the structure of the universe through time and space they have reached the big bang theory. That's where all matter, energy and time "was" one - all reduced to a single point where the universe began. It doesn't matter how we measure and analyse the universe, if we go deep enough, or far enough, we find the truth, which is undivided wholeness. This single point from where the big bang emanated is called a singularity. From this we can conclude that the universe is one 'thing' right now because everything that exists now was created from a single point of infinite mass and density. If the universe was one thing at that point then it is still fundamentally one thing now because the infinite present moment contains the total flow of all phenomena.

The singularity is the fundamental unified state from where everything derives. The universe experiences itself from many perspectives and as many objects but it is always only one process, on the fundamental level, with no opposites or duality, just like the wave of probability or singularity. For the singular continuous universe to have conscious awareness then something has to look at something else. That's what normal everyday conscious awareness is - the ability of the universe to look at itself and its subjective place within itself (i.e. our individual self). The universe experiences itself as separate conscious entities looking at many other separate conscious entities and objects. The universe creates the self (i.e. ourselves) to perceive itself (i.e. the environment around ourselves) and perceive itself within itself (i.e. become self-aware). However, by discovering the true nature of the singularity within the big bang theory then we can understand the illusory nature of ourselves as a fragment of the whole and know that we actually are the whole. From this perspective, it is possible to dissolve the illusion of the separate ego and become aware of the continuous universe (i.e. the singularity). This is where all points of consciousness manifest from, and out of, one point, where all phenomena emanate, including the self that we identify with.

Another way to see very deeply into the true structure of the universe is to look as far down into the smallest structures of matter at the sub atomic level, i.e. quantum mechanics.

Two slits

Physicist and philosopher, Neils Bohr, alongside famous names from Werner Heisenberg to Einstein, vastly expanded modern theories in quantum mechanics in the early part of the twentieth century. It was reinterpreting the results of the Double Slit Experiment, and in developing the Copenhagen Theory that the structure of the quantum world was reimagined around the concept of probability. The experiment saw individual photons of light travel, one at a time, through either one, or other, of two slits in an impenetrable sheet. Photons of light are the smallest indivisible component parts of light. Within this experiment photons of light are fired from a "photon gun" at a barrier which they can't pass through. However, the barrier has two slits in it which the photons can pass through. Beyond the barrier there is a photon sensitive screen, and when a photon hits the screen, the exact location where the photon hits the screen can be detected, measured and recorded. The results were unexpected. It was thought that photons of light were tiny particles of matter like bullets and if this were true then the pattern that the photons would leave on the screen would be a pattern that corresponds to the shape and size of the slits. However, instead of getting the pattern on the screen of light particles being like separate bullets of matter, they got what's called a wave interference pattern.

To illustrate how this pattern gets generated we have to imagine that the barrier with the two slits and the screen are being suspended in the surface of a pond of water. Then, instead of the photon gun, imagine that we drop a stone in the water at the location of the photon gun that would cause a ripple in the water. That ripple would hit the barrier with the two slits in it. That one wave would then ripple out through each slit making two separate waves traveling towards the screen. Those two rippling waves would then interfere and blend with each other and would then hit the screen generating the wave interference pattern. So, it seemed that light is waves but it didn't make sense because they were firing separate individual particles of light. They thought that maybe the light particles were somehow waving all together as one entity. They thought that this could be happening because they were firing so many photons at once. To see if this was true they developed the capability of firing just one photon of light at a time through the slits, so each time they fired one photon they would get one point they could measure on the screen, like one bullet hole. One bullet hole would suggest that the light particle was one point of matter. However, as they continued to fire photons one at a time, the overall pattern of all of the points from each individual photon on the screen created the interference wave pattern. This was shocking because it means that the photon of light is one bit/fragment of matter when it is fired and it then turns into a wave and travels through both slits at the same time, interferes with itself as a wave, and then turns back into one particle again to leave a single point of measurement on the screen (like a bullet). This was astonishing because it didn't seem to make any sense that the photons were particles and waves simultaneously.

So, to try to find out what was going on they created a photon detector (i.e. a sensitive camera) that they could place at each slit to measure which slit each photon was passing through on its journey to the screen. Maybe this would reveal some insight as to how the wave interference pattern was still being generated. The result was even more astonishing and baffling because when the scientists put detectors at each slit to measure the photon of light then the light stopped being a wave and acted like a bullet of matter. Each photon then passed through one slit at a time and the pattern on the screen corresponded to the size and shape of the slits. If they took the detectors away then they got the wave interference pattern but if they put them back then they got the pattern of separate particles. It was a wave until they looked and then it was a particle again. This process of the wave turning into a particle is called the 'collapse of the wave function' in the Copenhagen interpretation of quantum mechanics. This is not just true that photons of light are waves until they are observed. It is also true that all atoms that make up all matter in the universe are waves until they are observed. So, it would seem that all particles and atoms are waves until we observe them and then they become particles of matter. When we don't look at the particles then they are waves which means that they are everywhere and nowhere in particular, all of the time, throughout the experiment. But, when we look at the particles with a measuring device then the particles are separate fragmented entities at a specific location in space and time in the universe.

If we believe that the secondary reality that we experience from the perspective of normal everyday consciousness is what really exists then we would believe that all atoms and particles are fundamentally separate fragmented bits of matter. From the perspective of this illusory belief the results of the double slit experiment make no sense and seem impossible. However, it does make sense if we understand the primary reality of the continuous universe as an enfolded unified flowing process that unfolds into the illusion of the fragmented universe. From this perspective, it makes perfect sense that an atom is always one continuous flowing wave. Every atom is everywhere and nowhere as a wave because every atom is one process containing all phenomena until we look and then we experience separate atoms where nothing separate actually exists. When the universe unfolds into seemingly separate fragments then the atoms have to be experienced at separate and distinguishable locations. For example, their location is somewhere on the spectrum of north and south, high and low, fast and slow etc. The universe has created the experience of itself as separate fragmented parts in order to become consciously aware of itself. This is localised spatial perception. The one wave of the universe is experienced as separate phenomena within normal everyday conscious perception when the universe observes itself via a conscious point of awareness (i.e. the conscious observer). This process manifests the experience of all separate atoms and events in the universe. Moreover, it is this same process that describes how the fundamental feature of consciousness (i.e. transpersonal free will), in relationship with matter, dictates the pattern of the separate phenomena that make up the experience of the fragmented universe. During spiritually enlightened consciousness we experience how these seemingly separate phenomena, that make up the fragmented universe, really equate to one flowing process.

Two slits around a galaxy

Theoretical physicist John Wheeler then took the double-slit experiment further. He came up with the idea of measuring streams of light photos from distant celestial objects called quasars. The light from these quasars originates billions of light years away across the universe, so when we look at them we are looking billions of years into the past. Wheeler proposed that along the journey that this light takes to reach us, the photons have to pass many galaxies and these galaxies produce large gravitational fields. The light will be bent from passing through these fields because light is bent by gravity. So, he proposed using the gravitational force produced by a galaxy in between us on earth and the distant quasar to fulfil the same role as the two slits in the previous experiment. This time, instead of the photons passing through one slit or another they will pass by one side of a galaxy or the other side. As the photons travel we can measure which side of the galaxy they have been deflected around.

A group of astronomers then carried out this experiment. They found that if they pointed their telescope to look towards one side of the galaxy then they could see all of the photon particles that had been deflected around that side of the galaxy. If they pointed their telescopes towards the other side of the galaxy then they could see all of the photons that were travelling around that side of the galaxy. However, when they did not look at the light as it travelled and instead set up a photo sensitive screen that detected where the photons landed here on earth as they arrived, then the results were exactly the same as the smaller double-slit experiment. The wave interference pattern was generated on the screen. This means that, each individual photon left the quasar as an individual photon particle and then turned into a wave, journeyed around both sides of the galaxy simultaneously, as a wave, and then interfered and interacted with itself, as a wave, and landed on the screen on earth. However, the difference between this experiment and the smaller double-slit experiment is this: because the quasar is billions of light years away, the journey that the photon has taken though space, passing by the galaxy, has already happened. It happened millions of years ago and when we look at it then we are looking far back into the distant past. This means that we can change the journey of these light photons in the past depending on how we decide to measure/observe them. If we look at them, and measure them with telescopes, then they all become individual particles but when we don't look and we only measure where they arrive then they turn into a continuous wave of probability. Wheeler called this experiment the 'delayed choice experiment' because the choice that the scientists make to measure the light as a particle or a wave is made after the light has already committed to its journey towards the measuring device.

This means that not only is normal everyday conscious awareness generating the illusion of fragmented atoms in space but it's also generating the illusion of fragmented time where the atoms exist in a series of fragmented moments from the past to the future. All atoms flow through all points in time simultaneously as a wave but when we look the atoms have a specific location along a timeline. Normal everyday conscious awareness also creates the experience of ourselves at a particular localised moment in this time line and at a particular localised point in space. This is localised temporal and spatial perception. When we look, then we evoke the universe as it is now and as it has always been within the infinite present moment.

Everything can only exist now. Normal everyday conscious perception and transpersonal free will is evoking the experience of the whole fragmented universe, out of the wave of probability, and manifesting all phenomena in this infinite present moment. In the process of the universe becoming aware of itself, the primary reality of one flowing wave (that everything consists of) is experienced as separate fragmented parts. This process of conscious awareness brings into being the illusion of all separate fragmented points in the universe like particles in space and moments in time. As theoretical physicist Julian Barbour encapsulates in an interview in 2019:

> *"The space of possibilities is all possible now's and we're lucky enough to be in one of them...what is inside my brain is not only this picture but all of these other nows that we think were in the past. So, they're all there at once in some sense...each of our instance is part of the totality of everything - is one manifestation of everything"*

> *"We shouldn't think about local laws of motion or what's happening in the brain because we're all parts of the universe. And I would say there is a law of the entire universe and everything that we do - we are just being carried along...by what the whole law of the universe does."*

> *"The passage of time is simply an illusion created by our brains."*

However, what he calls a law, I called transpersonal free will because things that operate under laws are fixed, ridged and predictable. But as we see with the double slit experiment, the universe is free to manifest any pattern of phenomena in space and time within the infinite present moment depending on how we, as the conscious observer, chooses to see it. This demonstrates the unrestricted nature and infinite possibilities within the continuous universe, unbound by laws.

Wave-particle "dilemma"

The wave-particle "dilemma" is a "dilemma" because within quantum mechanics photons and atoms behave as both waves and particles at the same time depending on whether we are looking at them directly or not. When talking about this Einstein said:

> *"We have two contradictory pictures of reality; separately neither of them fully explains the phenomena of light, but together they do."*

It seems like a dilemma for us from the perspective of our localised perceptions because in order for self-awareness to exist then the continuous universe experiences itself as separate things like atoms. However, within the double-slit experiment we can know what atoms are in their primary reality of wholeness in the form of waves by indirectly measuring how they travel without actually looking at them. Normal everyday conscious perception evokes a universe where matter and events happen at different points in space and time. This is required in order for the universe to experience itself subjectively. But in reality, all things and events are one process. The wave-particle "dilemma" only exists because in the double slit experiment we can see beyond the optical delusion of separate particles created by normal everyday consciousness and we can know photons as the one flowing wave that they truly are. When we use detectors to directly measure the photons then we can only measure the photons at different stages of the experiment. This means that we have to choose which part of the photon's journey that we want to measure from firing the photon, the photon going through the slits, or landing on the screen. It is this act of measuring, i.e. observing and imposing transpersonal free will on the photons journey that creates the separate fragmented stages of the journey where no separate fragmented stages actually exist. All possible stages of the photons journey exist simultaneously as the pure potential of the one wave. The fragmented universe is evoked as an experience when the one wave of probability splits within normal everyday consciousness into observer and observed by the process of the universe becoming consciously aware of itself and, thereby, imposing transpersonal free will on all phenomena. By realising that the photon is one whole wave at the fundamental level of reality we can understand that the fragmented universe is a secondary manifestation of the primary reality of wholeness. Every stage of the photon's journey contains the whole journey as one wave of probability. It is normal everyday conscious perception that evokes one fragmented part of the journey out of the single process of the continuous universe. When we dissolve the mind phenomena that construct the illusory interpretation of ourselves as a separate individual (i.e. our sense of self), and our identification with the fragmented universe, then we can awaken spiritually enlightened conscious perception and become this wholeness. This is when our awareness expands to encompass much more than the illusory boundaries of our constructed individual self.

Causality

Causality or Cause and Effect is simply described as one event causing another event just like when one billiard ball hits another billiard ball and causes it to move as described by Newtonian laws of motion. Cause and effect is common-sense within our normal everyday conscious experience because it is a tool that we use every day in our lives and it works. That is to say that we use causality to make guesses to predict possible outcomes in the future. By looking at any situation and all of the possible variables that could influence what happens next, we can roughly guess what is going to happen in the future with some success. It is also how we can create our stories from the past to the future, for example: "I worked hard in school and that's why I'm successful and if I continue to work hard I will become more successful". The hard work is the cause and the success is the effect. Or "The invention of the internet caused a huge rise in communication technologies". Here's a story of cause and effect:

A person strikes a match and the flame from the match causes a house to burn down.

It seems common sense that the match was the cause and the house burning down was the effect. The reason that this is an illusion is because we have to isolate these two things and events (i.e. the match striking and the house burning) as separate fragments of the whole universe to make the story work which is impossible. Everything in the universe causes everything else in the universe simultaneously. All events in the universe flow like the water in a river. Therefore, one ripple on a river was not caused by a previous ripple. All of the water moves and causes the rest of the water to move simultaneously. There is no past that causes a future because everything is causing everything right now. This is demonstrated in the delayed choice experiment where photons of light are observed traveling around a galaxy. Because, by looking at the photon waves in the past then we change them into particles. Therefore, demonstrating that the chain of causation, traveling from the past to the future, is an illusion.

Imagine that each event is a wave on the ocean and the direction of time is the direction that the waves are traveling. All of the waves appear to be traveling in a direction along the ocean's surface but there is no forward or backwards on the ocean's surface because the ocean, as a total body of water, isn't moving. The water always remains in the same place. Waves are the patterns on the surface that create the illusion of motion by rippling in a certain direction. The motion of the waves is a secondary reality and the primary reality of water is wholeness which flows everywhere and nowhere because the ocean is fundamentally, one whole process. The apparent movement of each wave is experienced because they move in relation to each other. That is to say that it is the motion of the totality of fragmented waves that causes the experience of relative motion between them all. If we apply this metaphor to causality then it may seem that one wave is causing the next wave to move but we know that this isn't true because the whole ocean is one flowing process creating all the waves simultaneously. It is the change in the pattern on the ocean's surface that we misinterpret as time passing as Julian Barbour states:

"Change is primary, time, if it exists at all, is something we

deduce from it."

Cat behind a fence

The philosopher and writer Alan Watts describes an analogy of a man looking through a slit in a fence in his book titled: 'The Book on the Taboo Against Knowing Who You Are'. This next section is a development of his analogy.

Imagine that we have spent our entire life time in an empty room. We have never seen the outside world. Now, for the first time we can finally experience the outside world but we can only experience it by looking through a narrow slit in a fence so our view is restricted. There is a cat walking back and forth on the other side of the fence. But, because of our restricted view we can only see the cats head, then, as the cat walks, we can only see its body and finally, only its tail. We've never seen anything outside of our empty room before and so we don't know what a cat is. We are trying to understand the cat, and the outside world, by only seeing the body parts of the cat at separate moments. By applying the principles of causality then we would look at these separate parts of the cat and we would deduce that the cat-head causes the cat-body and the cat-body causes the cat-tail. Our observation would prove this "fact" to be correct. Every time we conducted this experiment, using the scientific method, it would prove causality to be true. From behind the fence, every time we see the cat-head we would predict the cat-body and we would be right. We would be able to predict the future from our point of view. But the obvious truth is that there is only one whole cat. However, it is our perception that is restricted so that we make the incorrect assumption that the cat consists fundamentally of three separate parts.

On the secondary level of reality, it is true that the cat is three separate parts in the same way that there are separate people on the earth. But at the primary level of reality there is only a continuous flowing universe, which flows through people shaped patterns that we are interpreting as separate people. The separate parts of the cat are an illusion. That is to say that we are formulating a misconstrued way of making sense of actual reality when we belief the cat is three fragments. Spiritually enlightened consciousness is equivalent to opening up the slit in the fence to experience the primary reality of the whole cat.

We can use this cat-behind-the-fence analogy to understand how it is that we see separate particles of light in the double-slit experiment when only one wave of light actually exists. By observing the universe without transcending normal everyday consciousness then we evoke separate fragmented things like a particle, a chair or a person out of one flowing process. In the same way, when we look at a cat through a slit in a fence without transcending our restricted perspective (i.e. the slit in the fence) then we evoke the illusion of a separate fragmented head, body and tail out of a whole cat.

Initially, the reason for conducting the double slit experiment was to study the smallest fundamental fragments of the universe and gather information about the tiniest "building blocks" of matter. However, instead of that, we discovered that the universe is one continuous wave of probability. The results of these experiments demonstrate that science has discovered the continuous universe and, therefore, spiritual enlightenment. That means it is possible to create a mainstream scientific model of spiritual enlightenment. However, we never will if we can't transcend the false assumption that the universe consists of separate fragmented parts. If we cling to the illusion of the fragmented universe then the results of these experiments will only cause confusion because they won't make sense from the perspective of normal everyday conscious perception. Then we will continue to search for answers in an illusion.

Wholeness and the implicate order

David Bohm has been described as one of the most significant theoretical physicists of the 20th century. The results of experiments in quantum mechanics led him to the conclusion that the universe is one indivisible process. He claimed that nothing could be separated into parts, and when we analyse any part of the universe then we can see the whole universe contained within it. He also said that Einstein's theory of relativity was pointing towards the same conclusion. He stated:

> *"The thing that quantum mechanics and relativity have in common is undivided wholeness. The view of relativity that Einstein was pursuing is that there's only a general field. Particles are concentrated regions of fields which spread out through the universe and merge with others, so the particle is an abstraction according to Einstein. There is only a whole field which is undivided."*

> *"In quantum mechanics, the whole universe is made up of indivisible links including the observer and the observed. So, they*

[relativity and quantum theory] both agree on that. So that was my starting point to say that the parts are abstractions from the whole. They have no independent existence".

"The particle is present in the whole and is merely unfolding and manifesting as a separate thing but it's actual existence is not separate. The particle is an abstraction due to our perception. Everything enfolds into everything and the entire universe is unfolding. This will provide a way of not only understanding quantum mechanics but bringing about a theory which would allow relativity and quantum mechanics to be particular theories with approximations within this more general theory."

As previously stated, Bohm's theory is called the 'implicate order' or the 'enfolded universe'. One analogy that he liked to use to encapsulate the principals of his theory was of a hologram. To create a hologram, we would need a holographic film with a holographic image on it and then we would shine laser light through the holographic film to see the projected image. But an astonishing thing happens with holographic film: If we were to chop it up into smaller pieces of film, and then shine the laser light through one of those smaller pieces, we might expect to see just a part of the original image, like with a normal film, but we wouldn't. In fact, we would see the whole image. Each fragment of the film contains an image of the whole. This is how Bohm illustrates his implicate or enfolded universe. It states that the primary whole universe is enfolded into every point in the universe and unfolds into the unfolded order or explicate order of separate fragmented parts. The explicate order is abstracted from the true reality of implicate wholeness. And so, fundamentally, there are no separate parts but only a continuous whole. He says that we can see this within quantum processes:

> *"Quantum process is indivisible. It can be broken but it becomes an entirely different process. Each process is a whole otherwise it can't be what it is. All the quantum processes are linked into one whole"*

He says that scientists break up the world into separate fragments and then there is confusion. There is confusion because the scientists assume that the fragment is a separate whole thing. Bohm believes that our primary focus on the concept of separation is the wrong concept to focus on and it is the result of classical physics. He states:

> *"In classical physics the parts are the primary concept and the whole is an auxiliary concept which is convenient when you have many parts working together like a machine but the parts are taken as the basic reality...But in quantum mechanics the whole is objective and the parts are the result of analysis. So, the whole is fundamental instead of the parts"*

Bohm believes that by focusing on the concept of the universe as a whole, and by not assuming division, then we can create a better way of communicating. He thinks that, although language labels the universe in terms of separate fragmented parts, we can learn to use language in a new way like poetry. This is what I would refer to as primary language which describes primary reality. Bohm's theory of the implicate order points to spiritually enlightened consciousness as he said:

> *"Everybody not only depends on everybody but actually is everybody in a deeper sense. We are the earth because all of our substance comes from the earth..."*

And on his enfolded universe:

> *"Mathematics itself suggests a movement in which any particular element of space may have a field which enfolds into the whole, and the whole unfolds into it. I call this the 'implicate' or 'enfolded Order' which unfold into the explicate order where everything is separate. In the implicate order everything is related to everything else. Everything contains everything. You are not acting mechanistically, as in being pushed and pulled by objects in the surroundings, rather, according to your consciousness of them, you act."*

Quantum entanglement

The science of quantum mechanics is the universe zoomed in and viewed at the distance of 10 billionth of a meter so particles can be measured. In 1981 a physicist called Alain Aspect proved through experiment, something called 'bells inequality' and this explained something called the 'EPR paradox'. What this means is that he discovered that particles can become 'entangled'. Particles become entangled when they "interact physically".

For example, when a laser light is fired through a certain type of crystal this can cause individual photons of light to be split into a pair of entangled photons. When two or more atoms become entangled they are then connected and always in relationship to each other. This means that when the two entangled particles are separated, even to opposite ends of the universe, whatever happens to one of those atoms then the opposite instantly happens to the other. Within science, this contradicts classical laws of physics and doesn't fit with causality and relativity as nothing should be able to exceed the speed of light but these atoms are communicating instantaneously across any distance. Albert Einstein called it "spooky action at a distance".

Just like with the double slit experiment and Bohm's Implicate order, quantum entanglement perfectly encapsulates the key principles of continuous monism. Everything is one process and everything is already entangled because all atoms have already existed at one point in space and time as a singularity at the big bang. That is to say that all particles and atoms are really one process as demonstrated by the theory of the big bang as they all originate from a singularity. Or, in terms of the Copenhagen interpretation of quantum mechanics: all particles are really one wave of probability, as illustrated in the double slit experiment. This means that all particles and atoms unfold from implicate wholeness (i.e. the continuous universe) into the explicate order (i.e. the fragmented universe) when they are observed and they become separate particles and objects from the true reality of oneness. In the same way, every photon of light is really one photon that is split into many entangled photons just like in the above example of the single photon that splits into two entangled photons when it is fired through a certain type of crystal. All particles and atoms in the universe are entangled from the process of the big bang (i.e. part of one indivisible process). This is illustrated with the metaphor of the water in a river. The whole river is entangled. It's one river all happening/flowing at once. It is an illusion of secondary language to say that our atoms were created a long time ago within a dying star. It is much truer to say that we are a dying star and the dying star is us right now as the process is entangled. Distance in time and space is an illusion generated by normal everyday consciousness.

This fact is explained in a paper published by Chapman university by physicists: Roman V. Buniy and Stephen D. H. Hsu that is titled 'Everything Is Entangled' and it states:

> *"We know from big bang cosmology that our universe was in thermal equilibrium at early times, and we believe, due to the uniformity of the cosmic microwave background, that regions which today are out of causal contact were once in equilibrium with each other...Typical states are maximally entangled and the approach to equilibrium can be thought of in terms of the spread of entanglement... The cosmological quantum state is likely to be typical...This implies a high degree of entanglement of particles, with the entanglement distributed uniformly..."*

General Relativity and Special Relativity

Einstein's theory of general relativity tells us that time slows down at a point in space where there is a stronger gravitational field (i.e. close to a large body like a planet) in comparison to a point in space where there is a weaker gravitational field. This is called 'gravitational time dilation' and is described on Wikipedia like this:

> *"Clocks that are far from massive bodies (or at higher gravitational potentials) run more quickly, and clocks close to massive bodies (or at lower gravitational potentials) run more slowly."*

The theory of Special Relativity tells us that time slows down at a point in space that is accelerating in comparison to a point in space that is not accelerating. To illustrate this there is the thought experiment called the 'twin paradox'. This consists of one twin sibling who flies away in a spaceship and accelerates through space in contrast to his identical twin sibling who stays on earth. When the twin in the spaceship returns to earth to join his twin he discovers that the non-accelerating twin sibling has aged much more because time slowed down for the twin who was accelerating relative to the non-accelerating twin.

Therefore, these theories tell us that time only slows down at a point in space next to a large celestial object like a planet or at a point that is accelerating in comparison to another point in space that is not near the large planet or is not accelerating. So, a person accelerating is only accelerating relative to another person, therefore, time is only slowing down for a person accelerating when they are compared to the time that is passing for a person who is not accelerating. That is to say that if they were both wearing synchronised watches then the person's watch who is accelerating would be ticking slower than the person's watch who is not accelerating.

So, the consequences of special relativity give evidence of the continuous nature of all phenomena and events in time because the speed that time passes at any point in space is dictated by all other points in space in a continuous network of connected transactions. That is to say that every part of the universe dictates what speed time travels in every other part of the universe because it acts as a whole process or a whole continuous field of space-time. This is hard for us to comprehend from our normal everyday conscious experience because we observe the time on our watch as objectively true. That's because we are looking from our illusory fragmented localised point in space and time. The time we experience from our perspective is an illusion in the sense that there is no objectively true speed that time ticks forward. There is only the whole pattern of all of the different points in space where the speeds of times ticking forward go at different speeds in a continuous network. All of these different speeds ticking forward make up the reality of the whole universe as they flow together as one inseparable process. Just like all of the waves on the ocean's surface cause all other waves simultaneously. Our perspective is from the illusion of one fragmented location in space and time which means that we only perceive the illusion of one isolated point in time.

By believing that the speed that our individual watch ticks at is objectively true then we are making the false assumption that our point in time is a separate fragmented place in time from the rest of the universe. There are no points in time in the universe which are separate from the whole flow of the universe. The time that we perceive from our normal everyday conscious perception is an illusion because of our localised spatial and temporal perception. Localised spatial and temporal perception is required for two or more conscious points of awareness to perceive each other as separate from each other in space and time. If the speed that our watch ticks really existed as an objective reality then it would not be possible to perceive it as ticking slower or faster depending on where it is being observed from in space. But it is. Craig Callender is a philosopher of science and writer of the book 'What Makes Time Special?' and he precisely encapsulates this idea when he writes:

> *"The universe may be timeless, but if you imagine breaking it into pieces, some of the pieces can serve as clocks for the others. Time emerges from timelessness. We perceive time because we are, by our very nature, one of those pieces."*

In a letter of condolence to the Besso family after his friend Michele Besso died Einstein wrote:

> *"For us believing physicists, the distinction between past, present and future is only a stubbornly persistent illusion."*

Secondary-language paradox

We experience the results of experiments in quantum mechanics and relativity as paradoxical because of our normal everyday conscious perspective. These paradoxes expose the flaws in our common-sense reasoning based on our misinterpretation of the universe due to this illusory perspective. These include the wave-particle duality of particles in quantum mechanics and watches ticking at different speeds as demonstrated with experiments in relativity. However, these paradoxes actually make perfect sense from a spiritually enlightened perspective.

Earlier I described the dualistic nature of secondary reality. For example, a magnet is perceived as two separate fragmented component parts (i.e. north and south). But, in primary reality north and south are two parts of one whole continuous spectrum of magnetism.

Similarly, we create depictions and descriptions of reality in our imaginations with the same dualistic qualities. These depictions and descriptions are our maps/stories of reality. When we describe secondary reality, we use secondary language which consists of dual concepts which are divided into polar opposites. In the same way that when we perceive secondary reality we perceive dual phenomena. When we describe primary reality then we use primary language which is a non-dualistic language. However, even the word 'non-duality' has an opposite - i.e. duality. Which means that primary language mustn't be confused with actual primary reality. Primary language is still only a conceptual description and not actual reality. Primary language can only point in the direction of primary reality. To demonstrate that the dualistic concepts within language can only represent the illusion of fragmented reality - here is an example of a sentence which contains a paradox regarding the concepts of truths and lies.

'This sentence is a lie.'

This paradox exposes the confusion that is caused by our common-sense. Our common-sense is generated by our belief that the reality, as we experience it, from a normal everyday conscious perspective, is real. From this point of view, we can't make sense of this sentence, because if it is true then it is false and if it is false then it is true. Therefore, using primary language, we can conclude that it must be true and false simultaneously. That is because the concept of lies can only exist in opposition to the concept of truths. Just as a magnet is north and south simultaneously or the mind and the brain are both one process of conscious awareness. We experience truths and falsehoods as separate phenomena but that is an illusion generated by normal everyday conscious perception. They bring each other into existence in our imagination.

An example that encapsulates this notion is found within the language of the Penan people in Sarawak, Malaysia. They have no word for 'thank you'. This is because the Penan people always share what they have with each other. 'Thank you' is an expression of gratitude for the choice that someone has made to be generous. But if people are always generous then there is no concept for thank you. The opposite of thank you would be an expression of disdain for a person who chooses not to be generous. Therefore, neither the concept of 'thank you' nor this type of disdain exists for these people. This shows that these two opposite concepts only exist in a continuous relationship with each other. In the same way that generosity can only exist in opposition to greed. We experience greed and generosity as separate phenomena but that is an illusion generated by normal everyday conscious perception.

Movement paradox

When we see a movie projected at the cinema the projector projects a series of still images and the movement is created by our conscious perception. We edit out the gaps in-between the still images in our minds. The gaps in-between each image lasts for 1/80th of a second, and during these times the screen is darkness, but our normal everyday consciousness creates the illusion of a smooth uninterrupted fluid motion picture. It was also discovered that if two lights close to one another flashed in a darkened room in quick succession, then what we perceive when we look at these two lights is one straight line of light traveling along from the first light to the next. This illusion of movement is called the PHI Phenomenon. In 1977 the philosopher Nelson Goodman wanted to know what would happen if the two spots of light were different colours. Scientists Paul Kolers and Michael von Grünau then investigated this question, and what happens is seemingly extraordinary. The person watching the two lights flashing still sees a point of light traveling in a straight line from the first light to the second, but halfway along the journey to the second light the colour of the light changes to the colour of the second light. The question is: how do we (i.e. the observer) know what colour the light of the second light is going to be before it lights up? It seems like we can see into the future? The explanation given by professor Daniel C Dennett is that the human nervous system receives the signal of the light flashing, and then the brain holds the information and makes a decision of how to perceive those two flashing lights. Then the perceiver experiences the interpretation of two flashing lights as a straight line of moving light. He explains it like this:

"...there is a crucial finishing line or boundary somewhere in the brain where the order of arrival equals the order of 'presentment' in experience because what happens there is what you are conscious of."

This is termed 'Cartesian theatre'. This means that everything that we experience has actually already happened and our nervous system is taking all of the information in the form of signals and then creating a kind of "movie" for us to experience. This shows how our experience of the world through normal everyday conscious perception is a constructed interpretation of reality, meaning that it is an edited and artificially contrived version of the total flow of the universe. Our nervous system edits down that total flow of information and turns it into an experience within our conscious awareness.

However, we can see from inconsistencies like this one that it is not the actual universe. It is analogous to a movie, a map or a metaphor of reality. We know this because the light must have already lit up, but our nervous system presents us with a reality as if it hasn't lit up yet. This process is to generate the illusion of a straight line of light, that changes colour halfway between the two lights. That's because the version of reality that we experience from our local perspective is an illusory representation of what really exists (i.e. the secondary reality of fragmented parts).

Zeno's arrow in time

In Zeno's arrow paradox, movement seems impossible. It states that if we observe an arrow at any one moment in time, as it is traveling through the air, then the arrow can only be in one place at the exact moment it is being measured/observed. Therefore, at any moment the arrow is motionless. It states on Wikipedia:

> *"If everything is motionless at every instant, and time is entirely composed of instants, then motion is impossible."*

From our localised temporal perspective, we perceive motion through the PHI effect that was previously described. A series of static images flash onto our retina and the brain then processes those still images and creates a moving picture to produce our normal everyday conscious experience of motion. This process is described by theoretical physicist Julian Barbour in his book 'The End of Time':

> *"I suggest that the brain in any instant always contains as it were, several stills of a movie. They correspond to different positions of objects we think we see moving. The idea is that it is this collection of 'stills', all present in any one instant, that stands in psychophysical parallel with the motion we actually see. The brain 'plays' the movie for us, rather as an orchestra plays note on a score."*

Therefore, we can describe the world as a series of still images and as a fluid motion picture simultaneously. The brain holds many still images at once and merges these still images to create the fluid motion of events in time. In primary reality, movement and stillness create each other as dual phenomena that combine to create the experience of motion. The still images constitute the motion we experience and the motion that we experience is constituted of still images in a transaction between both phenomena. Just like north and south create the experience of magnetism. If we try to measure movement or stillness as phenomena that exist separately and independently from each other then we get the paradox of Zeon's arrow.

Zeno's arrow in space

From our local spatial perspective, the movement of an object is created by a transactional relationship with all other objects in space including ourselves. Whether or not we perceive an object to be in motion, and how fast we perceive it to be moving, is dictated by the motion of the objects we compare it to.

For example, imagine that we are standing on the earth's surface and measuring the movement of an arrow traveling through the earth's atmosphere at one hundred miles per hour. We measure it at one hundred miles per hour because we are measuring its movement in relation to our location on the earth's surface. Now imagine that we are standing on the moon's surface and we use a telescope to observe/measure the movement of the same arrow. We would now measure the speed of that same arrow as traveling at thousands of miles per hour. That's because we are measuring its movement in comparison with our location on the moon's surface. The moon and the earth are moving at thousands of miles per hour relative to each other as they travel through space. And so, by changing our location then we change the speed that we measure the arrow relative to ourselves. The point is that any object, at any point in space, can be described as motionless, or moving at any speed, depending on which other objects we compare it to in space.

Movement, as we perceive it, as a separate and independent phenomenon from stillness, that can be fragmented and measured at a particular location in space, independently from other objects, is an illusion. In the same way that the perception of the speed that our watch ticks, as a separate objective independent speed, at our location, is also an illusion. In reality, the speed that our watch ticks is dictated by all other points that watches tick in space. Localised temporal and spatial perception means that we perceive movement or stillness as opposite fragmented phenomena. We see the flaws in this assumption when we analyse and understand paradoxes like Zeno's arrow.

Hallucinating everyday

One reason that the illusion of normal everyday conscious experience seems real is because our individual experiences have consistencies between them. That is to say that because, for example, metal feels hard to me and if I ask somebody else if metal feels hard to them too, then they can confirm that it does. The fact that we agree on this seems to be evidence that metal is objectively hard. Now imagine that two people ingest a hallucinogenic drug and they both have the same hallucination that metal is soft. Now they both agree that metal is soft. This now means that the fact that metal is soft would be as objectively true as the fact it was hard when we were not under the influence of the hallucinogenic drug. We could argue against this notion by saying: "when we are on drugs we are hallucinating the reality that we are experiencing and a hallucination is not real." But the truth is that our normal everyday conscious perception is a hallucination. That is to say it is an illusory representation/interpretation of actual reality. Just as the image on a TV screen doesn't represent the reality of the process that creates the image on the screen. So, our normal everyday conscious experience doesn't represent the primary reality of the universe. The experience of secondary reality is a manifestation of the total processes of primary reality. Just as the image on the TV screen is a manifestation of the technological processes within the TV. Our brain chemistry and nervous systems are configured in a very similar way to one another so that we can experience a very similar hallucination of reality. Our nervous systems have evolved this way so that we can navigate through our subjective worlds together but what we experience isn't necessarily objectively true. We can prove this by ingesting hallucinogenic drugs and changing our perception of reality. Then, when we test the validity of this new perceived reality, we find that it is just as valid and real or unreal as the reality that we perceived without ingesting the drug. This may seem counter intuitive but we can logically deduce why it is true.

Our nervous system is a measuring devise. It measures and filters the information from the whole universe and constructs a subjective reality for itself. This is the process that creates our normal everyday conscious experience which manifests as an interpretation of reality whereby, we are the subjective observer looking out at the fragmented universe, and one of those fragments is ourselves. It is the universe measuring itself and, from those measurements, it evokes itself as a separate subjective individual experience (i.e. the self) and as an environment to experience itself within. We evoke hardness out of metal. We evoke particular aspects of the universe by editing the totality of information. We evoke the whole universe as fragmented objects in space and time and we evoke ourselves as a fragmented object with a local point of consciousness within the fragmented universe.

We can also see this illusion of subjective reality illustrated by examining the differences between our nervous systems and those of other species of animals. For example, the nervous system of a bat hallucinates a different aspect of the universe by perceiving reality in a very different way to the reality that we perceive and experience. Bats "see" sound. Bats "see" the shape and texture of the world using sonar and so they use sound waves to build a subjective picture of the world around them. We can't imagine the world they are creating because we evoke a visual world from light photons. Bats are hallucinating a different reality to us. If we were to reconfigure our nervous system and sense organs to make our nervous system create our subjective experience out of sound then we would see the same world as them. But neither worlds are truer than the other, our nervous systems are just creating different subjective realities.

As is described in Donald D. Hoffman's 'Interface Theory of Perception'. The reality that we are hallucinating is useful for our survival in the same way that the interface/screen on a computer is useful for navigating the total flow of information within the computer. However, the interface/screen doesn't represent what actually exists within the computer and doesn't tell us what a computer really consists of. In the same way that our experience of from the perspective of normal everyday consciousness is the experience of the interface/screen (i.e. secondary reality). Within this metaphor, spiritually enlightened consciousness is the experience of the circuitry within the computer (i.e. primary reality). From a spiritually enlightened perspective we can understand/experience how the illusory secondary reality of the images on the screen (i.e. normal everyday conscious experience) get created. That is to say, if we learn how the circuitry (i.e. the continuous universe) works, then we can understand how the illusory reality of the fragmented universe is manifested within our normal everyday conscious perception. In a lecture Richard Dawkins describes how our brains have evolved to create notions and experiences like solidity so that we can navigate through our world:

> *"Our brains have evolved to help us survive within the orders of magnitude of size and speed which our bodies operate at. We never evolved to navigate in the world of atoms. If we had our brains probably would perceive rocks as full of empty space. Rocks feel hard and impenetrable to our hands precisely because objects like rocks and hands cannot penetrate each other. It's therefore useful for our brains to construct notions like solidity and impenetrability. Because such notions help us navigate our bodies through the middle-sized world which we have to navigate."*

Chapter Four: What's the meaning of all this?

The frequency of enlightenment

"A man in an elevated spiritual state uses rhythmically articulated signs, begins to dance, or sing...The performing of this act we are referring to – self-penetration, exposure – demands a mobilisation of all physical and spiritual forces of the actor" - Jerzy Grotowski (theatre director, theorist and writer)

To understand the truth of something fully and deeply is to truly understand its meaning. However, to understand the meaning of anything we can only describe it in contrast to its opposite. For example, we can only describe dark as opposite to light. The real meaning of anything can only be found in the totality of all phenomena (i.e. the continuous universe). But it's impossible to define the whole universe because it has no opposite to define it in contrast to.

What is the meaning of the universe? The answer to this question is not found within language because language has the same problem as describing anything within the universe. Language is a conceptual description of reality and the concepts in language only exist in contrast to the opposite concepts. The only way to answer the question of the meaning of the universe is to experience the answer directly. Meaning that you can't experience the terrain by analysing the map, no matter how long and hard you study the map, the only way to experience the terrain is to walk through the landscape. That is to say that the only way to experience what's real is by transcending the map of our illusory individual selves, and experiencing the real terrain of the universe in the infinite present moment, i.e. spiritually enlightened perception. We can only use language to describe the experience but the meaning is not within the language, it's within the experience. To describe the experience of spiritual enlightened conscious perception we must contemplate something that has intrinsic meaning that transcends any description.

Contemplate the meaning of music. Imagine listening to a piece of music that elicits a profoundly meaningful reaction within you when you listen to it. The reaction that I'm referring to is not merely the emotional reaction within yourself but more than that. I am referring to the actual meaning of the music. Now imagine that after you have finished listening to this music a person walks into the room who couldn't hear the music. This person has never listened to this piece of music before and they ask you: "What's was the meaning of that piece of music that you were just listening to?". This question is impossible to answer. You could try and describe the meaning by saying something like: "It made me feel sad, it was slow in tempo and got faster." This conveys nothing what so ever about the meaning. It's a redundant question because the meaning of the music can only be experienced by listening to it. It would be like somebody who has never had a sense of smell asking you: "What does a rose smell like?". The answer is that a rose smells like a rose as defined by all other smells. We experience the meaning of a piece of music when we experience the meaning of a piece of music and we can't describe this meaning. When describing the meaning of being a great martial artist Bruce Lee famously said:

"It's like a finger pointing away to the moon. Don't concentrate on the finger or you will miss all the heavenly glory"

The finger represents language and the ego-story as the abstract description of reality that can only point towards the heavenly glory of the experience.

Returning now to the meaning of music: We can see how we focus on the ego-story and language (i.e. the finger) when we imagine a musician playing an instrument and while they are playing they are constantly analysing the process in their mind by thinking things like:

"What is the next chord? The next chord is B flat, then C major, then B minor. Then what's next? I wish I didn't play that last section like that, I got it wrong, I should have played that better. What's next?".

They continue to think like this until they get to the end of playing the piece of music and they then realise that they didn't experience the music. The meaning of the word music is: 'a sound that produces beauty'. That beauty has to be experienced for it to mean anything. In this example, the musician didn't experience the meaning of their own action. They were lost in a world of the abstract future and past. They were regretting what they had just played or were thinking about what they were about to play next. They were focusing on chords and notations which are symbols that merely represent the music, just like conceptual language merely represents reality. Moreover, if they are playing only for the intention of gaining a future reward in the form of money, fame, status etc. then they are not playing music for the sake of experiencing music. They remain lost in the identification of themself as an individual within an abstract story within their imagination which blocks the experience of primary reality.

We know how it feels to experience the meaning of a piece of music. We have phrases that describe this. We say things like: "I was lost in that piece of music". Think about what this sentence is conveying. When we say ""I" was lost in that piece of music" then we mean the "I" was lost. Meaning that we (i.e. the self) dissolved. The local individual perspective vanished. In Bruce Lee's language, the "finger" was lost and all that was left was the "heavenly glory". We may say something like: "I lost myself in that music" or "I forgot who I was when I was experiencing that piece of music". This is all conveying the same description of the dissolution of the illusion of the self. However, losing ourselves does not mean that we become none existent, because our sense of self, our thoughts and our emotions are also a manifestation of the totality of phenomena i.e. the continuous universe. Therefore, when we lose ourselves in the music, then ourself becomes one with the true reality of flowing oneness, without the illusion of ourselves as a separate entity.

Contemplate the seemingly clichéd lyrics contained within a lot of dance music. The lyrics often contain very similar phrases, such as: "Let the rhythm move your body" or "Let the music move your soul". These lyrics encapsulate the experience of ego dissolution because ego dissolution includes the dissolution of the sensation of personal free will. These lyrics describe the meaning of dance. That is to say that the rhythm of the music is moving our bodies and our bodies are moving the music in one continuous flowing process. We experience the truth that we are not personally or individually choosing the dance moves that we enact. Our awareness expands into transpersonal free will, which is beyond our personal volition, and encompasses our continuous relationship with the rhythm of the music.

We will eventually transition back from this state of ego dissolution, i.e. being lost in the music, and into normal everyday conscious perception again when we start to identify with our ego-story once more. That is to say that thoughts arise in our mind that create a narrative for us to identify with again. These thoughts may include: "I didn't like the last dance step I just did" Or "How should I move next?". Or "am I doing it right?" or "I regret how I was just dancing" or "I want to be better at dancing" or "I want that person to like my dancing." Then we are dancing to fulfil an abstract future fantasy and the true meaning of our dance, as the expression of transpersonal free will in relationship with the rhythm of the total universe in the infinite present moment, is hidden by the illusion of our separate sense of self.

Music or dance is its own meaning. It has no opposite. Music is the pattern of the dance between dual opposites. The dance is between the transpersonal free will of consciousness on one side, and the randomness and predetermined processes of matter and events on the other. It is the dance of the single continuous process of consciousness and matter that manifests out of the formless vibrations of the wave of probability, to create the rhythms, frequencies and patterns of all forms including: atoms, particles, thoughts, objects and entities including ourselves. It is the experience of the illusory boundaries of ourself dissolving into the melodies and harmonies of this process of continuous wholeness. There is no conceptual or abstract definition of the meaning of the music, dance and, therefore, the universe. We can't know the meaning of the universe because we are the meaning of the universe because we are the universe. Michael Meade is an author, and scholar of mythology, anthropology, and psychology. When describing the role of dance within mythology Meade says:

> *"Dance is a metaphor for being alive in life. We're all supposed to be dancing."*

Within a book on contemporary Hinduism, by the author: Satguru Sivaya Subramuniyaswami, which is titled 'Dancing with Siva', it states:

> *"The Cosmic Dance describes the Hindu view of existence...Dancing with Siva is everything we do, everything we think and say and feel, from our seeming birth to our so-called death. It is God and man forever engaged in sacred movement"*

Also on Hinduism, the scholar of mythology: Richard Stromer wrote an essay titled: 'Shiva Nataraja: A Study in Myth, Iconography, and the Meaning of a Sacred Symbol', Stromer writes:

> *"In the image of Shiva Nataraja, I find a deeply moving symbol of the ultimately mysterious and paradoxical nature of the divine. Creation and destruction, order and chaos, asceticism and sensuality, immanence and transcendence, life and death, being and non-being all coexist, balance, and, indeed, dance with each other in Shiva's divine choreography. Most wonderful of all, Nataraja shows us that these eternal oppositions and*

dualities can never be reconciled into some neutral third or middle position... The very nature of our experience of the numinous, resides precisely in the inherently irresolvable, irreducible nature of all the eternal paradoxes so magnificently manifested and celebrated in Nataraja's cosmic ballet."

Suspended existence

The dancing symphony of the whole flowing universe is contained within all phenomena. Therefore, the experience of spiritually enlightened conscious perception and ego dissolution can be facilitated by the experience of any object or the engagement in any activity. Within positive psychology, the process of achieving ego dissolution and reaching spiritually enlightened consciousness during an activity is called 'flow state' or 'being in the zone'. It is described as a completely energised and joyful absorption and emersion in an activity, resulting in the loss of our sense of space and time (i.e. the loss of localised temporal and spatial perception). It also results in the failure to attend to our own basic needs such as eating and sleeping as well as the loss of our reflective self-consciousness. This means that our analytical thoughts disappear and only our actions remain, uncriticised and unjudged by our internal monologue as our inner voice is no longer present.

Flow state was named by Psychologist Mihály Csíkszentmihályi in 1975. It was called flow because people describe the sensation of flow state as like being carried along by the flow of water (i.e. the sensation of being moved by a force other than our own personal free will). To illustrate this phenomenon, think of a great champion of a sport, such as formula one racing. When they reach a state of flow they seem to have superhuman reflexes far beyond the capabilities of the other competitors. When an interviewer then asks them how or why were they able to reach this level of speed and efficiency, they reply with the same types of answers, such as: “In that moment it was just instinct”. If they are asked what was going through their mind during the race they will reply with something like: “I wasn’t thinking anything. It was just happening. It didn’t feel like I was doing it, I couldn’t think in that moment, I haven’t got time”. The Formula One driver Ayrton Senna, during qualifying for the 1988 Monaco Grand Prix, said:

> *"Suddenly I was nearly two seconds faster than anybody else, including my team mate with the same car. And suddenly I realised that I was no longer driving the car consciously. I was driving it by a kind of instinct, only I was in a different dimension. It was like I was in a tunnel."*

Former 500 GP rider Wayne Gardner, talking about his victory at the 1990 Australian Grand Prix, on The Unrideables 2 documentary, said:

> *"During these last five laps, I had this sort of above body experience where I actually raised up above and I could see myself racing. It was kind of a remote control and it's the weirdest thing I've ever had in my life. After the race...Wayne Rainey said: "How the hell did you do that?" and I said: "I have no idea.""*

They experienced their true nature of transpersonal free will in a continuous relationship with the flow of all phenomena by reaching a spiritually enlightened state of consciousness/flow state. This seems strange to us if we identify as an individual with personal free will. They both describe how it was instinct and that they didn't know how they were doing what they were doing. In the same way that we don't know how we are beating our hearts but they keep beating. While racing at that speed, it would not be possible for their rational minds to label the experience and create abstract narratives (i.e. an ego-story) out of the information. That is to say it would be impossible to think "I will break at this point and now I will change gear and then I will look towards the next corner" because there isn't time to translate what is happening into language and narratives while performing in flow state. In the same way, we haven't got time to translate the process of speech in terms of each movement of our mouth. The physical process of speech is happening beyond our knowledge because it is a reflexive and flowing consequence of our transpersonal free will. This feeling is in contrast to the feeling of personal volition during normal everyday conscious experiences. Because, during normal everyday conscious experiences, we experience the sensation of planning our actions before we act. This gives us the delusion that we, as separate individuals, are controlling the process of the action. However, the sensation of planning our actions is also part of the flow of transpersonal free will in relationship with all phenomena.

I'm not saying that personal free will does not exist. I'm saying that it doesn't exist separately from all other phenomena. All other phenomena, including our physiological processes, other conscious minds, natural physical systems etc. influence our personal free will. And because we are entangled into one process with all of these things, therefore, it means that they all go together to constitute our transpersonal free will which contains our personal free will.

Senna and Gardner also describe how their localised spatial perception altered from their normal everyday conscious experience of looking from their usual point of view to looking through a "tunnel" or from "above" their body. Senna said, "I was in a different dimension. It was like I was in a tunnel" and Gardner said: "I had this sort of above body experience". This illustrates that our localised spatial perception, that gives us the misconstrued perspective of ourselves as a separate individual looking out at the world from a fix point in space is not an accurate interpretation of what we are on the primary level of reality. The change in Gardner's and Senna's spatial awareness illustrates that awareness is not confined to a fixed point of view. Awareness actually encompasses far more than our perspective during normal everyday conscious experiences, and we can expand into this unrestricted awareness when we reach flow state/spiritually enlightened conscious perception.

During their training, they may say things like: "Be one with the car" or "Be one with the road." This is because, in a deeper sense, they are the car and they are the road, and so by saying this they can trick themselves out of the illusion of being separate from their environment. When a driver experiences flow then they "know" how to drive and thoughts about how to be a better driver dissolve. In the same way that an oak tree "knows" how to be an oak tree and doesn't need to think about how to be a better oak tree. The racing driver, in flow state, "knows" how to drive in the same way that a swallow "knows" it's way from the UK to a specific branch on a tree in Africa. The difference is that the driver has to transcend their sense of self as an individual to reach their full potential in the present moment. Whereas every bird or tree reaches their full potential spontaneously within every lifetime. However, we, as individual humans, have a much greater range of behaviours available to us than a bird or a tree. Achieving instinctual and innate mastery over a behaviour such as racing a car is called 'unconscious competence' in positive psychology. The driver, the swallow and the oak tree are one with the flow of the totality of all phenomena manifesting as their behaviour in the infinite present moment. Even the learning process of the driver, whereby the driver consciously remembers past races, to plan to be a better driver in future races, is all happening in the flow of the whole universe within the present moment.

We all "know" the way in any moment and during any endeavour. We may argue against this notion by saying that a racing driver hasn't always been a "good" driver. We may say that they used to be a "bad" racing driver until they practiced, a lot, and finally became a good driver. However, an oak tree grew from a small tree into a big tree but it was always perfectly fulfilling its role as an oak tree at every moment of its growth. The tree was never "bad" at being a tree, it just grew. It was always one with the total process of nature and the universe and couldn't be bad at being a tree or need to improve. However, by focusing on an imaginary journey (i.e. the ego-story) that doesn't exist, then we create a fiction of not being good enough and needing to be something else or somewhere else. That illusion blocks the experience of flow state and the experience of our true nature as the whole process of transpersonal free will in relationship with all matter and events at every moment. That is to say that we can't be more than what we already are at every moment.

During an interview for the 1999 documentary titled: 'Choke', the Jiu-Jitsu master Rickson Gracie describes his flow state like this:

"You just allow yourself to go like an automatic pilot. You don't

know exactly where you're going until the movement happens. Because you cannot anticipate what's going to happen. You must allow yourself to be in a zero point, in a neutral point, and be relaxed and connected with the variations. So, you pretty much go with the flow. This is a point beyond the knowledge. It's years and years of playing around to give you this kind of sensibility."

During a lecture in 2004 called 'Flow', Mihály Csíkszentmihályi quotes a composer who is describing his experience of flow when composing music:

"You are in an ecstatic state to such a point that you feel as though you almost don't exist. I have experienced this time and again. My hand seems devoid of myself, and I have nothing to do with what is happening. I just sit there watching it in a state of awe and wonderment. And [the music] just flows out of itself."

Here Csíkszentmihályi explains the reason for the composer's experience:

"his body disappears, his identity disappears from his consciousness because he doesn't have enough attention (like none of us do) [to] really do well [at] something that requires a lot of concentration and at the same time to feel he exists. So, existence is temporarily suspended."

It is the experience of ourselves as a separate point of awareness with an ego-identity that is suspended during flow state.

The death delusion

Where do we go when we die? This question is the same as asking: where does my fist go when I open my hand? Let's answer that question. If we make a fist now with our hand and look at it then we have just witnessed a fist coming into existence. Now, we can give the fist an identity as an individual. To do this we could describe this fist as manly, butch, aggressive, a fighter, dominant and many other qualities that we associate with this fist. Now give the fist an ego-story. For example, we could desire that this fist uses its aggressive nature to fight injustice in the world. Now we can open our hand and ask ourselves: "where did this fist go?". It's a legitimate question. The fist was there, it did exist but now it's gone. We could now grieve the loss of this fist and its identity. Obviously, we would never grieve for the loss of a fist but it's the same principle as our own existence and annihilation as a separate individual. That is to say that we don't feel loss when the fist disappears because we can see and experience the fundamental truth that there is a whole hand. We know that the whole hand makes thousands of different shapes and patterns including fists. The fist can't have an existence that is separate from the hand. We created the identity of the fist in our imaginations by giving the fist a story of its existence, for a certain amount of time, and we gave names to its characteristics. But to say that the fist is a separate process from the whole hand would be delusional. The only reality that exists is the reality of the whole hand including every pattern that the hand makes. This is how we are generating the illusory identity of ourselves as separate individuals within a story.

The whole universe is flowing to create all phenomena simultaneously in the form of infinite patterns of phenomena (i.e. atoms, energy, vibrations, fields and forces etc.). We are identifying as one small pattern of phenomena within the totality by labelling this small pattern as our self by imagining ourselves within a separate story and then identifying with that story. From the perspective of primary reality, every birth and death is really our birth and death. In this sense, we, as a separate individual, never die because we were never really born. It is our mind phenomena that generates the delusion of ourselves as a separate conscious individual that dies. It is our ego-identity, constructed from our particular ego-story, made from our desires and regrets, our hopes and fears, that creates our imaginary sense of self that all dissolves and dies. Our true nature as the whole continuous universe that is expressing itself as infinite possible people and entities, including ourselves, in the cosmic dance between opposites, including consciousness and matter, can never die. And so, in this sense, nothing can die apart from this particular way in which we are imagining ourselves to be. When describing spiritually enlightened conscious perception Eckhart Tolle said:

> *"Die before you die. Go into it deeply. Your physical form is dissolving, is no more. Then a moment comes when all mind-forms or thoughts also die. Yet you are still there - the divine presence that you are. Radiant, fully awake. Nothing that was real ever died, only names, forms, and illusions."*

When two become none

During sex, the two people are a literal physical illustration and embodiment of the continuous process of all things, as they flow together and create one pattern from what seems separate. The duality of male and female, self and other is revealed as two parts of a continuous whole. When two become one process, continuous with all phenomena, via their complete psychological and physical union, then they have achieved spiritually enlightened consciousness. When we reach flow during sex our egos dissolve and the pure bliss of existence remains. Then we are not "doing" anything but sex is happening. However, if the egos remain present during sex then the sex will be a game of trying to satisfy desire. In this case sex becomes a mechanical thrusting, rubbing and fondling with a conceptual objective of some sort like status or gratification in the future. This leads to self-consciousness, over thinking, anxiety and an inability to connect to the moment. In turn, this will inhibit the ability to experience pleasure by, for example, causing erectile dysfunction in the man and the feeling of not being present with the other person. This leads to self-critical thoughts like: "I'm not very good at this. I need to be better" which can further block the experience of the present moment.

Oceans of awareness

Our ego-identities take a lot of effort and energy to create and sustain. Much of our lifetime is spent reflecting on our imagined past and contemplating what actions we should take that will result in a better imagined future. We hope that the decisions we make will lead to less suffering and more fulfilled desires for ourselves in the future. This constant conceptual and abstract thinking to construct and maintain our ego-identity can be exhausting. We could argue that we need the ego-story in order to "get stuff done" in the present moment. However, as we can see from the examples of Senna and Gardner, we can perform in a much more efficient way when we transcend the-self and dissolve our ego. That's because, from a spiritually enlightened conscious state, we have access to all of the energy that we usually use to create and maintain our sense of self.

In order to find relief from our fictional narratives we are instinctively drawn towards experiences of spiritually enlightened consciousness. For example, one of the most popular holiday destinations is a trip to the seaside. We sit or lie down facing the ocean and watch the waves. Every day, millions of us choose to experience the waves in our free time. Like with music or dance, the pattern of the waves doesn't have any logical reason to keep rolling in and out against the sand, so we cannot incorporate their motion in to our story. Any pattern which is moving for its own sake can facilitate the experience of the continuous universe.

As with the example in chapter two, when I described the act of observing a pigeon while meditating, to illustrate the possibility of achieving a state of awareness whereby we can become the witness of our external and internal world, (i.e. our mind and environment) flowing as one. And, when this occurs, then the distinction between our inner and outer worlds dissolve. As a result, we experience that both worlds are a united process. That is to say that we can dissolve the imaginary boundaries in our mind that creates the experience of separation between ourselves and the environment. This liberates us from the experience of ourselves as a separate conscious individual. Our awareness then expands to encompass a lot more of the universe. In the same way, when we experience the rhythm of the ocean waves, united with the rhythms of our own physiological and psychological processes, we become aware of our entangled and continuous relationship with the patterns and systems of nature. We become aware that we are those systems and patterns.

Experiencing the ocean waves, like music, facilitates the transcendence of our normal everyday state of consciousness because of the multiplicity of physical forces, sights and sounds that emanate from the crashing waves. The energy of each wave is in a continuous process with the entire ocean, the gravity of earth and the moon, the atmosphere and the meteorological systems of the planet.

However, if we focus on a conceptual description of the waves then we will remain within an abstract story. This is the story of ourselves watching the waves rather than experiencing the true reality of our continuous relationship with the waves. For example, if we say "I am enjoying this experience. The waves are so beautiful" we will remain within secondary reality where we are an observer looking at the separate phenomenon of the waves. This reality is conveyed within the Chinese philosophy of Taoism. It highlights the way of being in harmony with nature by not naming it. It emphasises the necessity of detaching from our desires and not naming our experiences in order to feel our true connection with nature because the Tao (i.e. the way) is indescribable. This sentiment is expressed within the main text, i.e. the Tao Te Ching or Daodejing, when it states:

道 可 道 非 常 道

"The Tao that can be told is not the eternal Tao"

名 可 名 非 常 名

"The name that can be named is not the eternal name."

An example of an individual who is connected with his true nature as expressed in Taoism is Wim Hof. Wim Hof, also known as The Iceman, is a Dutch extreme athlete and creator of the 'Wim Hof method'. He is well known for many extreme feats of endurance, including withstanding freezing temperatures for long periods of time. His method involves breathing techniques and exposure to very cold water. These techniques have given him, and those who follow his method, the ability to "control" their body's autonomic nervous system which, by definition, was believed to be outside of our conscious control. However, by getting into freezing water and with controlled breathing techniques he can dissolve his ego and reach spiritually enlightened conscious perception to connect to the totality of his physiological systems.

The idea behind his method is that the intense stress of the cold water activates a reaction from our autonomic systems to keep us warm. We don't usually experience this reaction because of the physical comfort that we have become accustomed to as a result of technological achievements in the modern world. The cold quietens the thinking mind, therefore, facilitating connection to the flow of the universe which includes our autonomic nervous system. So, by practicing this method we gain the ability to trigger the autonomic nervous system, at any moment, by expanding our awareness into our transpersonal free will. However, it is not the individual who is triggering it. It is the process of letting go of the illusion of the individual self that allows us to align with the innate power of our full physiology. This is when our awareness expands beyond our illusory personal free will and individual conscious self to encompass transpersonal free will and pure consciousness.

Wim Hof, and others who follow his method, have the ability to trigger the autonomic immune response, and this ability has been tested under scientific conditions. For example, they have been injected with the endotoxin - E-coli. This would usually make a person extremely ill for several hours after the injection. However, Wim Hof and the followers of his method were all able to trigger their own autonomic immune system to fight off the infection. Therefore, they developed no symptoms of illness due to the injection.

We can understand this process of ego dissolution by listening to Wim Hof's descriptions of the process in an interview in 2019. He encapsulates what it means to act from a spiritually enlightened perspective and not from the perspective of the illusion of the self. For example, at one moment, the interviewer asks Wim Hof a question from the perspective of his own ego (i.e. from identification with thoughts) and Wim Hof replies from the perspective of spiritually enlightened consciousness and ego-dissolution. That is to say that Wim Hof describes how he has to "let go" and feel his connection to something deeper (i.e. the continuous universe, including transpersonal free will) to achieve "control" over his autonomic systems and not, as the interviewer wrongly presumes, by thinking.

> *Interviewer: "When you're going into the meditative state, you know you've just been injected with the endotoxins, what are you visualising? What are you actually thinking when you are trying to get into adrenaline or bone marrow or...?"*
>
> *Wim Hof: "If you go into the ice you're not thinking about your*

mortgage or your wife or this or that...You feel. The focus will be on your feeling and how to get this feeling into adaptation and how to overcome whatever is coming. And it goes directly. The cold has been my teacher. I just follow the teacher - the feeling, and learnt to let go...I felt it, the connection was there, beyond any words. That's what I was looking for. I was tapping into deeper parts of the brain, feeling pure energy, feeling power, innate capacitated power...It's all in the mind - learning to let go in the right way. Following your breath. The breath is able to prime the body, and then the neurology of the mind. If I'm able to make my skin temperature not go down while being exposed to ice cold water, that's power, and that power is the same power we can learn to embrace and awaken which will tackle any stressor in the world...In the cold you shut up, and all this turmoil - emotional confusion - the broken heart, it's all physical. It's all real. The cold is able to shut it up, shut it down, and survive."

Double bind: try not to try

Experiencing our true reality as a continuation of the one process of the universe, by watching the movement of the ocean, is an act of meditation resulting in ego-dissolution facilitated by the waves. However, if we 'try' to experience this meditative state then we will fail to get there. That's because, in order to 'try' to experience it then we are trying to get to a desired future within our ego-story. Therefore, our effort reinforces our identification with our ego-story and blocks the spontaneous experience of being continuous with whatever we are focusing on. Within meditation practices, the words that are used to facilitate the achievement of a meditative experience are 'surrender', 'acceptance' and 'letting go'. To surrender and accept something is to let go of trying to achieve it and, therefore, be one with the present moment where we experience our continuous nature with all phenomena. Anytime we 'try' to meditate then we are defining ourselves as not experiencing our continuous nature with all phenomena now. We may then end up in the frustrating situation where we are 'trying not to try' which is an impossible paradox. Also, the words in our mind misdirect us back into identification with our ego-stories. For example, if we think "I can't meditate, this is stupid" or "I need to surrender to the flow". This is an ego-story with an imagined version of ourselves in the past who is not spiritually enlightened and there is an imagined version of ourselves in our desired future who is spiritually enlightened. However, if we surrender and accept this process of identification with an ego-story then all of these thoughts will also be experienced as the flow of the continuous universe and transpersonal free will.

We are in a continuous flow with the totality of phenomena all of the time because we can't be anything else. It is the experience of the delusion of the-self that hides the experience of our true reality/essence. Therefore, acceptance of the experience of the continuous universe is just acceptance of what is already true - acceptance of what we already are.

There are meditation apps and books available to help guide meditators through a vast array of spiritual practices. However, these products have got to be sold to consumers. Advertisements are used to sell these products and these adverts contradict the core principle of meditation. They say things like: "Do you desire a healthier lifestyle?" Or "Do you want to have more focus? Meditation can give you more focus and make you healthier". Relaxation and health are future desires in our ego-story. Therefore, this will only further entrench us into identification with our stories. This is the opposite of achieving a meditative state because there is no future purpose for meditation. Meditation is to sit and to exist, to accept and surrender. Sit for the sake of sitting. Exist for the sake of existing. We are the entire universe so we don't have anything to achieve. We can't not be good enough. We can never get meditation right or wrong. We can only delude ourselves into thinking we are doing it wrong or that we are not good enough. We are everything that has ever been achieved or will ever be achieved right now in this moment. Meditation for a purpose other than meditation is not meditation. Our thoughts, feelings, opinions, regrets and desires will come and go like reflections rippling on the surface of a lake or like each breath in and out, so let them. Let everything happen and be all of it. Only then can we expand awareness into transpersonal free will beyond the illusion of the structures of our ego and be happy and healthy. Not because we desired happiness and health but because we let go of the structures of our ego and mind phenomena that created our sense of self and our desire for happiness and health in the first place.

Melting disparity

Love, empathy and kindness are essential core components of spiritual enlightenment. This is because conflict with others is only generated in a dualistic world of opposite phenomena including: enemies and allies, wrong and right, good and bad, or moral and immoral. When only one united universe is experienced in a state of spiritually enlightened consciousness then conflict can't exist and only true love and kindness remains. The love that we search for from the perspective of our ego-identity, which I will call 'self-orientated love', is found within our imaginary future. Therefore, because 'self-orientated' love is imaginary it directs us away from the experience of 'unconditional love' or 'spiritual love' which is the essence of the undivided universe.

Self-orientated love can only exist in our ego-story in opposition to hate so the self-orientated love we feel for someone can flip to the feeling of hate for them. We feel self-orientated love for a person who matches our criteria for what constitutes a loveable person within the fiction of our imagined future. These may include: loyalty, trust, respect, sexual attractiveness, money, fertility etc. We project this self-orientated love on the person because they bring us pleasure, sex, status, power, riches, children, companionship or whatever meets our criteria within our ego-story. Then when the person changes or their situation changes or they exhibit behaviours that don't fit with our idea of what we love, then our love starts to change into hate for them or for the relationship or for the situation. For example, if they aren't as rich as we thought or they get fat and less attractive to us, if they stop having sex with us or they cheat on us or they lose their job or discover that they can't have children then our pleasure may turn to pain, attraction to repulsion, happiness to sadness, desire to disgust, contentment to resentment and our love may turn to hate. To continue feeling self-orientated love for them after these "negative" changes then we could change ourselves, by changing our criteria, which is possible but difficult, and may require therapy. If it was unconditional/spiritual love that we experienced for this person then we would love them regardless of their actions, physical appearance or circumstances.

Unconditional/spiritual love transcends the secondary reality of duality and conceptual descriptions. The spiritual love we experience between ourselves and significant others is a focal point for a deep meditation. It radiates and permeates through our life as we experience our continuous oneness with the whole universe facilitated by our total psychological and physical entanglement with them. Spiritual love is the experience of the melting of disparity replaced by the pure bliss of undivided existence. Love is the absence of separation. It is when the illusory boundaries between our self and another self dissolves.

A mother usually experiences unconditional/spiritual love for her child. This is because the mother experiences herself as one entity with the child as the child grows from, and is continuous with, her substance. By embodying the creative process of the universe and manifesting another conscious entity from her own physical form she experiences the truth - that oneness is the fundamental reality of all individuals. She and the child become the embodiment of the indivisible process of growth and decay, of life and death. She experiences the true reality of the continuous interconnectedness of living creatures and of being one flowing process with all people on the level of primary reality. Then the birth facilitates the experience of the illusory surface level of secondary reality - of the division of one person into two or more. However, the process of the growth of the child within herself remains a source of connection to the continuous universe which manifests as her unconditional/spiritual love for the child.

"Mother is the name for God in the lips and hearts of little

children" - William Thackeray (novelist)

The stagnation of creativity

When the American comedian Dave Chappelle was being interviewed by fellow comedian Jerry Seinfeld in 2018 he gave an analogy which described the difference between his creative process when it's going well as opposed to when it's going badly:

> *"The idea says: "let's go" and I say: "Where are we going?" and the idea says: "don't worry, I'm driving" and then you just get there. Sometimes I'm just in the trunk but the idea takes us where it wants to go. And then there's other times, there's me as my ego who's like: "I should do something." But there's no idea in the car so that formula doesn't work."*

Here Chappelle describes the consequences of acting from the confines of our ego-identity verses acting from an expanded awareness that encompasses transpersonal free will. Within Chappelle's metaphor, for an original creative idea to become fully realised then the ego has to stop driving the car and let the idea drive. This is the same as saying we must let go of personal free will and stop trying to control our journey. That is to say that we must go with the flow of the idea which is dictated by transpersonal free will in relationship with physical events within the infinite present moment. When we surrender the illusion of personal control over the idea then the ego falls away and we can realise something truly original. Our ego-story is a useful tool to get from one imagined place to another but when we believe that our ego-story is real then we remain limited to within the imaginary boundaries of our ego-identity (i.e. what we already know). In reality, we are continuous with an infinite universe of possible ideas which we can only access when we stop limiting the definition of ourselves to a fictional story. The only way for us to be truly original is to surrender personal control of our destination by letting go of the steering wheel. In primary reality, we, as a separate individual, were never actually driving the car, we were only pretending to drive because of the illusory sensation of personal free will. Which is a required component of the useful tool which is our ego, i.e. our imagined version of ourselves.

When we don't 'let go' of our ego-identity then we can only regurgitate ideas that already exist within our ego-story and, therefore, have already been imagined. Real creativity occurs when we stop resisting our true reality and allow new ideas to flow through us by experiencing spiritually enlightened conscious perception.

As young children we have much more of a natural capacity for creativity than as adults because when we are children we accept the reality of the present moment, as we experience it, without judging it. As children, before we have constructed our dogmatic ego-identity, we are free to express ourselves without the constraint of maintaining the illusion of our individual self. That is to say that we don't yet have an imagined story of ourselves within a past and a future, so our experience of reality in the present moment is unedited and unrestricted by our conscious mind. As our sense of self grows, we slowly create an ego-story and ego-identity, but before this happens we experience a state of pure awareness which is aligned with transpersonal free and the infinite present moment. This means that, as children, we are open to the infinite potential within us to be anyone we want to be, at any time, without limitations, in the infinite present moment, and so we have access to unlimited creative inspiration. This is important, as it means that children have the ability to construct any ego-identity to fit into the culture and environment where they happen to be born and where they must thrive and survive.

When we play, at any age, from this state of unrestricted awareness (i.e. flow state), any competition with each other becomes irrelevant, or of secondary importance, because competition only exists within our ego-story. Competition (i.e. striving to win in our imagined future) is a useful tool but when we stay connected to the present moment then we play much more effectively because we are free from our story and, therefore, free to play any game that occurs to us, in new and original ways. The game will manifest effortlessly and spontaneously because we're not trying to play it for any reason other than the joy of playing it. The play specialist – Fred Donaldson calls this type of play - 'original play'. When he was describing how this type of play transcends our identification with our ego-identity he said:

> *"Play provides a way for us to slide between the categories in which we live. In that magical time/space, which is play, we're not members of any category. We aren't men or women, white or black, Americans or South-Africans. That's the genius of play, not to be limited by all the categories. Once you experience play and then find yourself back being male, white, and all the other cultural labels, you realize that here is an experience that can take you beyond all the cultural limitations you have accepted*

about yourself. You discover that there is a way to slide between all of the frames the culture has imposed."

We can experience the limitlessness and innate capacity for originality in every form that manifests in the universe free from the imposition of maintaining a sense of self. For example, every snowflake crystallizes as an intricate and perfectly unique pattern that is distinct from every other snowflake that has ever existed or will ever exist. That's because they don't have an ego-identity so they can't identify with a story of crystallizing in a particular pattern in their imagined future. They can't look at another snowflake and copy that snowflake's pattern or desire to be a particular pattern so that other snowflakes will think they are more beautiful.

When we experience spiritually enlightened conscious perception we become a receptacle for the expression of the boundless patterns of nature. Original play facilitates our authentic impulses of transpersonal free will. In contrast, by utilising our ego-identity for inspiration, our creativity is then based on our memories and conditioning to achieve an imaginary future that we believe that we desire. Then the art that we produce is based on a preconceived idea of what we imagine will be "good" art. Then the art is inauthentic, repetitive and contrived. That is because authenticity comes from the expression of transpersonal free will within the infinite present moment beyond the illusion of the self.

The majority of the mainstream entertainment that we consume is a commodity created from a preconceived notion of what is "good". Good, in this sense, is defined as popular and profitable because money is the metric that we use to judge the worth of the art that is created. This type of art and entertainment is popular because, while we identify with our ego-story, we desire more of what we already identify with. Therefore, because mainstream art feeds our ego-identities it mainly consists of repeated patterns. Meaning that we consume art that we have already incorporated into our identity because it reinforces our self-image and identity. This is 'unoriginal play' - when we try and perform what we think is good rather than creating art for its own sake. When we base our creative inspiration on our ego-identity then our authentic impulses are stifled and creativity stagnates. In his book 'The Empty Space', English theatre director Peter Brook describes the process of an actor whose creativity is based on his ego-identity:

> *"He is reaching inside himself for an alphabet that is also fossilized for the language of signs from life that he knows is the language not of invention but of his conditioning. His observations of behaviour are often observations of projections of himself. What he thinks to be spontaneous is filtered and monitored many times over."*

When we experience our authentic impulse, we say we have found our 'calling' in life because it calls to us (i.e. it found us when we stopped trying to find it). This is our authentic destiny realised - when we experience ourselves as the flow of pure awareness and transpersonal free will rather than as a story that we must force to turn out how we imagined it "should" turn out. Our authentic creative impulses occur when we experience ourselves and our story as a manifestation of the dance of transpersonal free will in relationship with the totality of physical processes and events. We block these impulses when we resist the present moment by forcing our imaginary personal will on the world. A willow tree absorbs the stress on its branches by bending with the wind instead of fighting against it. If the branches of a willow tree tried to resist the wind they would snap. This illustrates the cycle of suffering that the identification with our ego-story produces.

In the Chinese philosophy of Taoism, spiritually enlightened conscious perception is described as Wu-wei, which means to act without intention, to yield and go with the harmonious flow of nature, and is often associated with water. It states that when we experience the divinity that is within us we achieve oneness with the universe and have been said to have reached 'Tao', translated as 'the way'. Elements of 'the way' that are emphasised include: naturalness, spontaneity, compassion, simplicity, humility and the accomplishment of non-action. Non-action being our authentic impulses without trying to impose our illusory personal free will on ourselves or our environment.

Chapter Five: Ethics and morality

The master of dreams

Although we may be able understand and accept that we are the whole universe experiencing itself subjectively, this understanding can reveal further unanswered questions. For example: why do bad things happen to us? This question arises because it may seem strange that we experience suffering at all if we are really one with the totality of phenomena. That is to say, why would the universe create suffering for itself? Here is an analogy which gives an answer to this apparent contradiction.

For this thought experiment, we must imagine that we are going to fall asleep tonight and experience an infinite number of dreams and, not only that, but we will have complete control over everything that happens in these dreams. This means that we can choose, using our personal free will, exactly what happens in every dream, including where we go, who we are, what we do, what everyone else does and what kind of dream-world we live in. Put simply: we are the God of these dreams. Whatever we wish for, at any time, will manifest. We may think that we would experience all of our desires in exquisite perfection within a flawless paradise because every detail of this dream universe is under our personal control. Each dream might have differences, if we want it to, but essentially, we would always choose for them to be pain free, stress free and blissful. We may think that, at the end of each dream we would tremble with anticipation at the thought of the next dream so that we could continue this ecstatic experience of pleasure and fulfilment. However, this is not the case, and in fact, these dreams would be a terrible nightmare. It is true that having personal control over everything in the universe is the only way to avoid suffering. However, when we make the assumption that we actually want to live in a world without suffering then we don't have a real understanding of what it means to suffer.

Suffering is created when our experienced reality does not match our desired expectations. That is to say that when the life that we experience is not the life that we wanted then we suffer. In these dreams, we are in total control of reality, therefore, we cannot suffer but this dream world, devoid of suffering, would be much much worse than a world which contains lots of suffering.

This is because the only controlling force in this dream universe would be our own personal free will. This means that the only events that could occur are events that we have already decided will happen before they happen. That is to say that we would be trapped within the limitations of our own personal thoughts and our own personal imagination with no random or determined events and no other autonomous conscious people, and, therefore, no transpersonal free will. As soon as we introduce those things into the dream-world then suffering can occur. So, for there to be no suffering, nobody in the dream can do or say anything that we haven't already decided they will say or do. It would be like living in our own scripted movie that we have already written before it plays out in the dream-world. It would be like writing every event and every line for every character in the dream, including ourselves. We would be trapped inside our own head, with no source of inspiration from anywhere other than our own individual conscious mind, constrained to within the boundaries of our ego-identity. Every conversation with other people would be a conversation with ourselves. After experiencing these dreams then we would quickly realise that we don't want to have complete personal control of everything. It would become obvious to us that we don't want to live in a world that is safe, predictable, with no challenges and nothing to learn from.

Therefore, we would want to change this stagnant dream-life. In this metaphor, we are the god of our dreams, so, if we want to surprise ourselves then we can. We would start having dreams that would unfold without our total control. So, we wouldn't know exactly what was going to happen next or what other people would say or do next and so on. We would want to experience a bit of unpredictability in the middle of this unoriginal and uninspiring world. Maybe not too much at first, we wouldn't want anyone to die but just a bit of uncertainty. This would mean that we would actually be choosing for there to be a chance that the future won't turn out how we want it to turn out. This would mean that we would be choosing for there to be a chance that we will suffer. This new, unpredictable dream may feel exciting and we may enjoy the challenge, or it may go wrong and we may suffer immense pain. But, we may learn and grow as a result of that suffering and we may become much more skilful at dealing with the next challenge. Or the suffering might be too much for us and we might want to wake up from the dream. Then, after a few thousand more dreams, we would want bigger surprises and bigger challenges.

Eventually, after many more dreams, maybe a hundred thousand dreams, maybe a million dreams, maybe ten million dreams, we will want to experience everything that can possibly be experienced. Remember that we will have infinite dreams. Therefore, eventually, we will find ourselves dreaming the exact life that we are living now. This analogy answers the question of why our life is the way that it is, and includes suffering.

Suffering is a fundamental component of the creative process of growth, change, adaptation, inspiration and leaning.

The belief that we want no suffering in our life is a misconstrued interpretation of what we actually want. This 'god-of-our-dreams' analogy illustrates that we do want to suffer and we don't want to control everything. We don't want our future to work out exactly how we desire. We want the universe to be an exciting and dynamic flow of transpersonal free will and physical processes which manifest as infinite possible realities including our own life. This means that we (i.e. our individual selves) don't actually want what we think we want. If we always got what we wanted then we would be trapped within the structures of our own individual mind. Therefore, it is good that the experience of our individual self and our personal free will, as a separate entity, is an illusion. It is good that the universe is a dynamic and creative process of flowing transpersonal free will in relationship with random and determined physical events, and we will always be one with this process. By accepting the events in the infinite present moment, as they unfold, including our own suffering, then we no longer suffer as we become one with the infinitely rich creative expression of the universe. We become free to be whoever we want to be, free from the suffering that is created from trying to make reality match a future that we have imagined in our ego-story. From this perspective, suffering is not experienced as suffering because it is part of the process of the infinitely rich creative expression of ourselves, as a point of awareness, that is continuous with all phenomena. Then we do have control because we are in alignment with transpersonal free will, which is the creative force of the universe that flows through us.

Levels of harmony

Here is another example of how to answer questions such as: why do bad things happen to good people? Or, why does the world contain so much pain, chaos and suffering? At the secondary level of reality, we experience our subjective individual self as separate from all other things. However, at the primary level of reality, everything is one continuous flow. A good way to illustrate these two realities is by thinking about the human body. When we zoom in with a microscope to see the smaller structures within our body we see a different world to the world that we see when we look at our body as a whole organism. Think about the activity at the microscopic level within our circulatory system. At this level of observation, to our eyes, it all appears to be in complete chaos within incredibly complex networks. As Bill Byson points out in his book titled 'The Body':

> *"In the second or so since you started this sentence, your body has made a million red blood cells. They are already speeding around you, coursing through your veins, keeping you alive. Each of those blood cells will rattle around you 150, 000 times, repeatedly delivering oxygen to your cells, and then, battered and useless, will present itself to other cells to be quietly killed off for the greater good of you."*

Within these microscopic systems millions of micro-organisms seem to be at war. Viruses, bacteria and fungus seem to be fighting for control. Blood cells are transporting vital nutrients, keeping our temperature and PH levels constant, carrying hormones, oxygen and carbon dioxide. White blood cells are creating antibodies to fight infections within an intricate continuous relationship with the lymphatic system and the immune system. Internal structures within cells are being destroyed and repaired millions of times per second. To our eyes it looks like a terrifying and complex fight that could all go wrong at any moment. Within any tiny section of the circulatory system, it seems to us, that there is a battle that can be won or lost in an instant. It looks like everything is at stake, as some component parts, like white blood cells and antibodies are fighting for "good", and some, like bacteria and viruses are fighting for "bad".

But we know that talking like this about the blood stream doesn't make any sense. There are no ethical or moral dilemmas taking place here. It is all just happening. It's playing out exactly how it is supposed to because when we zoom back out again and view the organism as a whole then we can see that there is perfect harmony and balance. It would be pointless for us to take sides in this fight. We would only disrupt the perfect natural flow of events that are taking place almost all of the time during the life time of a human organism. This analogy of the levels of the human body is useful for trying to understand all of the chaos in the world on the scale of individual humans and trying to figure out why "bad" things happen to us (i.e. why we suffer).

When we fight for one side verses another (i.e. good verses bad) and the bad side wins (i.e. we don't get the reality we wanted) we suffer because our ego-story had not turned out how we desired. But really, when we zoom out to the fundamental level of primary reality, then we experience that the flow of events and phenomena, governed by transpersonal free will, randomness and determinism are required in order to have a process that has the capacity for infinite possible realities. Even the phenomena that we define as bad, that causes suffering, plays a vital and fundamental part in the potential of the universe to manifest as any and all realities. This isn't to say that we shouldn't fight against suffering and injustice but to understand and experience this suffering as a key component of creative growth, change and learning. Rather than as a fight to achieve a desired future.

The suffering that we inflict on each other is generated from trying to accumulate pleasure, statues, wealth and power etc. in the future of our ego-story and not connecting to what is real (i.e. primary reality). By accepting, and becoming continuous with the creative flow of transpersonal free will and letting go of the illusion of our separate individual self, then we will not have the need to focus on achieving a desirable imaginary ever-receding future for ourselves at the expense of others. Instead, we will connect to an infinite present moment of continuous loving oneness which encompasses all individuals and nature. From this spiritual perspective, conflict, hierarchy and status is revealed as an illusion of the fragmented universe. That is to say that the enemy that we're fighting can only exist if we exist in order to fight with them. We are the same. We are on the same spectrum of difference as our enemy, we require each other to exist because we are continuous.

Suffering from a fragmented life

From a spiritually enlightened perspective we experience the primary reality of the continuous universe. From here we are able to surrender and be at peace with our suffering, and the changes in our lives, and experience them as the creative fuel, that can propel reality into any possible pattern within the present moment. The alternative to this is to remain confined within the illusory boundaries of our individual self and the ego-story. From here we will experience an endless cycle of needless conflict, an unquenchable desire for wealth or success, a lack of peace of mind and the inability to connect to the present moment. This will result in a lack of fulfilment, which will manifest as perpetual suffering for ourselves. However, it is worth reiterating that there is a beauty and a utility to our stories, memories and history that should be appreciated and honoured. But, when we misinterpret the story for actual reality, that's when we become trapped in the illusion. There is a folk tale that illustrates this point perfectly. It is the story of a wise old man who accepts the flow of events in his life from a spiritually enlightened perspective.

The wise man lives with his son on a farm and their most treasured possession is their horse. One night their horse runs away. All of the villagers say to the old man: "How terrible and unfortunate that your horse has run away!" and the wise man calmly replies: "maybe". The next night the horse returns with a whole herd of wild horses and the villagers say to him: "How wonderful and fortunate that your horse ran away and brought all of these horses to your farm!" and the wise man replies in the same calm manner: "maybe". The next day, whilst the wise man's son is taming one of the wild horses, he falls off the horse and breaks his leg. This means that he is no longer able do any of the farm work and the wise man is too old to do it himself. The villagers say: "How terrible and unfortunate that your horse ran away and brought all of those horses back to your farm for your son to then break his leg trying to tame!". The wise man replies: "maybe". Then their country goes to war and it is a legal requirement for all men to go and fight. However, because the wise man's son has broken his leg, it means that he can't go to fight in the war. The villagers say to the wise man: "How wonderful and fortunate that your horse ran away and brought all of those horses to your farm for your son brake his leg trying to tame so now he doesn't have to go to fight in the war!". The old man replied: "maybe".

The point is that our normal everyday conscious perception is so restricted that when we look from our individual point of view we have no way of experiencing the continuous nature of events. And, as is illustrated in this folk tale, we can't even see the consequence that just one event will have on another event. Therefore, we certainly can't see how one event fits into the totality of events and how they are a manifestation of transpersonal free will. We don't know what it really means for the son to break his leg because, from the perspective of our individual sense of self, we can't see what the implications are of this event on all other events in the entangled network of events. When we look at the universe from our normal everyday conscious perspective and judge one fragmented event then we are judging something that doesn't really exist. One event only exists within the continuous flow of all other events in relationship with transpersonal free will. Therefore, the idea of feeling sad or happy because of the outcome of any fragmented event, separate from its relationship with other events, is absurd.

The ability to strive for a better future in our ego-story is a useful and beautiful capability of our imagination because it motivates us to achieve success (i.e. survive) and form an identity. However, suffering because of the outcome of one event makes no sense because we don't know which events are negative or positive because we don't know how they all fit together. The wise man is at peace all of the time no matter what happens. If he had judged each separate event as good or bad then he would have spent his time worrying and suffering by, either wishing things had gone differently or hoping things would be better in the future. Instead, he was able to accept reality as it unfolded in the present moment without judging it and, therefore, transcend his ego-story. From this spiritually enlightened perspective his actions in the present moment are more effective as he is engaging with reality rather than his imaginary ego-story. Our identification with the fragmented universe prevents us from transcending normal everyday consciousness and reaching a spiritually enlightened perspective, where we can achieve flow state, unconscious competence, align with transpersonal free will and experience joy within our endeavours.

Future simulations

From our normal everyday conscious perspective, any change in the present moment which kills the possibility of a particular desired future makes us suffer. This is because, when the possibility of an imagined future dies, part of ourself dies with it. However, when one possible future story dies we don't experience complete ego-death because there are many different stories that we identify with to generate our sense of self. When we lose one of our narratives we then grieve the loss of this part of ourself (i.e. this one story line). We must then create/reimagine a different story line in its place.

This experience of the death of part of ourself is an opportunity to experience spiritual enlightenment because we can then observe how we construct our next imagined future. By observing the process of the creation on our new imagined future we can experience that the previous future, we were imagining, was never real to begin with. When we experience this then we no longer identify with the story because we see that it has no reality outside of our thoughts.

The wise old man didn't identify with a desired future and so he didn't suffer from the trauma of it dying. He always accepted and surrendered to the flow of changes in the present moment and adjusted his identity according to these changes.

The next story that we imagine and desire and identify with will seem just as important, valid, and desirable for ourself as the previous one. This is proof that no future that we imagine for ourselves is more right, real, true or desirable than any other because we can replace one with another. Shakespeare wrote:

"There's nothing either good or bad but thinking makes it so"

Epictetus, the Greek philosopher wrote:

"What really frightens and dismays us is not external events themselves but the way in which we think about them. It is not things that disturb us but our interpretation of their significance."

Buddha said:

"Our life is our creations of our minds, with our minds we make the world."

We identify with a specific ego-story because it's integral to our imagined existence as a separate individual perceiver (i.e. a self). Tribalism is defined as a group/tribe/society/family/community/nation which share an ego-story (i.e. a future) that they desire within their collective imagination. Identification with a particular ego-story as a group is what manifests as a cultural identity and a way of life for the group. In this context, our past is our traditions and our future is our political ideals. Because we perceive our own imagined ego-story as more valid, correct and desirable than any other, it means that we're in conflict with the ego-stories of other tribes and individuals. This is the bases for our prejudices.

Our prejudices give us the desire to try to persuade or force others to identify with the same ego-story as us. A tribe or individual that dogmatically identifies with an ego-story will try and destroy the ego-stories and cultural identities of other tribes and individuals. This is for two reasons. One reason is that if the two imagined futures of two group identities are perceived as unable to mutually co-exist, then each imagined future is a threat to the other and so they are in conflict. The second reason is, just like with political ego-stories, we need to oppose contrasting ego-stories because we define ourselves in opposition to others in order to bring each other into existence in the illusion of a dualistic universe. When we fight against each other's ego-story then we will push each other into more dogmatic and ideologically extreme identification with our desired future. The more extreme, dogmatic and ideological our ego-identity is then the more we will be willing to kill or die for our desired future. We are in conflict with each other over who has the most desirable abstraction to identify with. Alternatively, from a spiritually enlightened perspective, each ego-story, culture and way of life that we imagine is just as valid or invalid as any other because they are ultimately fictitious depictions or descriptions of reality.

During a talk called 'The surprising science of happiness ', Dan Gilbert talks about what he calls our 'experience simulators'. Our experience simulators are our different imagined futures that we believe will either make us happy or unhappy. They are analogues to our ego-stories. He states:

> *"A year after losing the use of their legs and a year after winning the lottery, lottery winners and paraplegics are equally happy with their lives...The research that my laboratory has been doing - that economists and psychologists around the country have been doing have revealed something really quite startling to us. Something called the 'impact bias' - which is the tendency for the simulator to work badly. For the simulation to make you believe that different outcomes are more different than they actually are. We see that winning or losing an election, gaining or losing a romantic partner, getting or not getting a promotion, passing or not passing a collage test, on and on, have far less impact, less intensity, and much less duration than people expect them to have."*

This illustrates how our ego-stories change as we identify with new imagined realities. It also illustrates how our biases and prejudices towards other people's ego-stories manifest. That is to say that if we identify with a capitalist-consumer ego-story then we would find it hard to believe that, if we were given the choice between either winning the lottery, or becoming paraplegic then we would become equally as happy with our lives regardless of which option we chose. But we would. After winning the lottery or becoming paraplegic we create a different ego-story and identify with that new story with just as much conviction as the old one. The more dogmatically we identify with our own ego-story then the more confused, angry, scared or disgusted we feel about the idea of identifying with contrasting ego-stories. For example, if we identify with a capitalist consumer narrative, then winning the lottery is a desirable future and so we will oppose the ego-story of a paraplegic who has not won the lottery as undesirable at best or as an abomination at worst in comparison. But, as we can see from the research, this perception is totally misguided. This evidence suggests that we synthesize our own happiness or unhappiness in our imaginations (i.e. in our ego-stories) regardless of actual reality.

To give another example: if we dogmatically identified with a heterosexual and/or masculine self-image we would then oppose a person who identifies with a homosexual and/or feminine self-image and declare that they are strange at best or an abomination at worst in comparison. We could think of infinite examples of these contrasting ideologies that are in conflict because of a lack of a spiritually enlightened perspective.

This conflict and prejudice is illustrated by the Anthropologist Wade Davis in a lecture that he gave when he talked about the cultural identity and way of life of the Maasai people in Kenya. Much of their culture has manifested as a result of the inevitability of regular droughts. He says:

> *"In the pastoral nomadic traditions of east Africa, particularly in the Chalbi desert of northern Kenya, drought is not some kind of cruel anomaly but rather a regular feature of climate, and surviving drought is a key imperative that allows a people to be."*

"The marvellous idea is that a single adaptive imperative: surviving drought, bifurcates throughout the entire culture and, in a sense, makes it what it is."

The Kenyan government thinks that they are helping the Maasai people by removing them from their nomadic culture by giving them a western education. They believe that this "modernisation" of these pastoral nomads is positive because it will increase Kenya's economic growth by creating workers for the "modern" job market. Wade Davis goes on to state:

"Pastoral nomads don't fit Kenya's image of itself as a modern state. So, as a result they go into school as a nomad, graduate as a clerk, can't go back, and going forward simply means to join an economy with a forty percent unemployment rate for high school graduates. They drift to the slums of Nairobi where they scratch a living from a cash economy. That looks, to the development paradigm, all for the good. Per capita income's gone up, urbanisation's gone up, literacy's gone up, but in fact quality of life has gone down"

"The other great myth is that somehow education lifts people out of poverty. On the contrary, the process of globalisation cements people into poverty. I have never, in my life, in traditional cultures, seen the wretchedness that one encounters around the periphery of almost any city in the so called third

world."

The Kenyan government's dogmatic identification with a global capitalist narrative means that a thriving economy is a desirable future and so they will oppose the ego-story of the Maasai people as an abomination in comparison. The Kenyan government sees drought as a negative force and not as a prerequisite and bases for a thriving culture. However, by making this preconceived and prejudiced assumption about the Maasai's culture they're killing a rich and unique expression of humanity. They're taking away the people's identity and forcing most of them to identify with an ego-story, and a way of life, which will create and maintain poverty for them. The Kenyan government see the Maasai people as a threat to their imagined future in their global capitalist ego-story and so they are trying to destroy the imagined future of the Maasai people and make them desire the same future as them.

The Philosopher and writer Robert Anton Wilson used the term 'reality tunnel'. Our reality tunnel is our restricted interpretation of the universe due to our subjective perspective within our ego-story that is limited to secondary reality. He says:

"There is no vantage point from which real reality can be seen. We're all looking from the point of view of our own reality tunnels. And when we begin to realise that we are all looking from the point of view of our own reality tunnels we find it is much easier to understand where other people are coming from. All the ones who don't have the same reality tunnel as us do not seem ignorant or deliberately perverse or lying or hypnotised by

some mad ideology. They just have a different reality tunnel and every reality tunnel might tell us something interesting about our world, if we're willing to listen."

From a spiritually enlightened perspective we see that all of the possible imagined futures and ego-stories flow together to create the rich tapestry of the totality of human possibilities. From a spiritually enlightened conscious perspective we're free to imagine any future for ourselves and for others without having any attachment to a specific illusion. Therefore, our identity and ego-story become fluid and unrestricted by any synthetic abstract reality within our imaginations.

Knowledge of the processes that generate our reality tunnels and ego-stories can give us insights into all of the possible ways that humanity can express itself within the total flow of phenomena. This can facilitate the dissolution of our own ego. Then we feel acceptance, empathy and tolerance towards other ego-stories and cultural identities. Obviously, if a group has the belief that they should commit violence on others then we must fight against this. But that fight is to maintain the balance of opposing forces in the world and not an ideological fight between one ego-identity and another. The feeling of tolerance that manifests as a result of transcending our ego-identity would not come from having a desired future of a more tolerant world. Desiring a more tolerant world would only mean that we have incorporated tolerance into our ego-identity. Then we would fight against people who are not tolerant and only create more intolerance by ironically being intolerant of intolerance and create more conflict. As with unconditional/spiritual love, true tolerance and true acceptance of others is the essential nature of spiritually enlightened consciousness. When we reach this enlightened state, just like the wise old man, we could accept differences and changes and we would never be the source of conflict or suffering in the world either for ourselves or for others.

Chapter six: Awakening pure awareness

Ayahuasca: death and rebirth

Ayahuasca is a psychoactive brew made from the Banisteriopsis Caapi root and the Psychotria Viridis plant. Dimethyltryptamine (DMT) is the main psychoactive ingredient. Ayahuasca is a traditional, ancient, visionary, psychedelic medicine that has been administered, within shamanic rituals for thousands of years, by the indigenous people of the Amazon basin in South America.

The anthropologist Wade Davis gave a talk called 'Dreams from Endangered Cultures' where he described the effects of DMT (Dimenthyltryptamine):

> *"…its's rather like being shot out of a rifle barrel lined with baroque paintings and landing on a sea of electricity. It doesn't create the distortion of reality, it creates the dissolution of reality…I argue that you can't classify these tryptamines as hallucinogenic because by the time you're under the effects there's no one home anymore to experience a hallucination"*

By saying "there's no one home anymore to experience the hallucination" he is describing the dissolution of the self. Just as Jim Carry said that you become the "universe experiencing a guy". Or as the composer who was quoted in Csíkszentmihályi's talk who said: "you feel as though you almost don't exist". Or as Ayrton Senna said: "I realised that I was no longer driving the car". Our ego dissolves and our awareness expands beyond the illusion of ourselves and into the continuous flow of transpersonal free will and physical processes. Wade Davis describes this as "being shot out of a rifle barrel lined with baroque paintings and landing on a sea of electricity".

Next, I am going to describe my own experience of being under the effects of ayahuasca. A problem that may be perceived with anecdotal evidence based on a drug induced experience (such as ayahuasca) is the belief that we can't learn anything from a hallucination because hallucinations aren't real. I would say that the opposite is true. The truth is that the experience that we are having of being separate individual perceivers in a fragmented universe during normal everyday conscious experiences is the deluded hallucination. Under the effects of ayahuasca we experience the primary truth of the continuous universe as spiritually enlightened states of consciousness are reached and the illusion of the self dissolves.

The psychiatrist and psychedelic researcher Stanislav Grof wrote this about the psychedelic experience:

> *"The main objective of psychedelic therapy is to create optimal conditions for the subject to experience the ego death and the subsequent transcendence into the so-called psychedelic peak experience. It is an ecstatic state, characterized by the loss of boundaries between the subject and the objective world,*

with ensuing feelings of unity with other people, nature, the entire universe and God"

I spent a week on a retreat in the Amazon rain forest in Peru, and during the course of the week I participated in four ayahuasca ceremonies, with eleven other participants. On the evening of each of these ceremonies we would congregate in one room where we would be joined by two shamans. After we had each drank our share of the brew we would lie down and the candle that was lighting the room was blown out. We were then in complete darkness apart from a slight glow from the light of the moon. Then we would wait for the effects of the brew to take place. Simultaneously, the shaman would perform rituals, songs, prayers, blessings and chants.

Firstly, it is worth saying that language seems truly insufficient at capturing my experience, however, it's all we have to communicate with so I will try.

Ayahuasca translates as 'vine of death'. Death occurs when the self dissolves which is when there are no remaining elements such as memories to identify with to construct our ego-story, so, we (i.e. the self) dies. This is not the same as taking a sedative, because in that instance our individual conscious awareness is suspended. But during the ayahuasca experience, the conscious mind of the individual perceiver becomes one with consciousness itself as conscious awareness expands beyond the conscious individual. During my ayahuasca experience, all of the things that comprise the delusion of who I am no longer had any objective reality. My ego-story, personal free will, localised spatial perception and localised temporal perception all drastically altered. At first, I violently battled to "hold on" to myself as I was trying to cling to who I think I am. I was straining to remember my life as it was melting away or reconfiguring into something else. I was shouting things like: "Make it stop" and "I don't want to die". My physical position in the environment and my spatial dimensions became fluid so, for example, in one moment I could be hanging from the ceiling a long way off the floor or I could sink through the ground as the room shrank around me. Things that were distant from me could now appear in the centre of me. The shape and size of my body mutated through many patterns.

Ayahuasca melted or transformed my thoughts, memories, fantasies, internal monologue, emotions and body and it warped the physical world that comprises my body and the world around me. Everything merged into a cacophony of colours, sounds and geometric patterns. Out of these patterns, many specific images and creatures would emerge and recede. For example, I would regularly experience the world from the perspective of some kind of reptilian or amphibious creature sitting on rocks by the ocean. Thoughts and feelings existed but were not "mine" anymore although they were still there. The objects, trees and plants around me would become conscious entities with awareness and sometimes I could see from their perspective. My external and internal world had no distinction, therefore, the Amazon jungle would often grow from within me or I would grow into the jungle to become one entity. I was living a multitude of new realities simultaneously and spontaneously.

The ego-story I had spent a lifetime creating crumbled away. I tried to resist this by using my rational 'problem-solving' mind to keep redefining myself. But the rational mind uses concepts such as self and other, or soft and hard as its building materials and it was these concepts that no longer had any meaning during this experience. The way I experienced myself in relation to the world made no rational sense anymore. Hot became cold,

old became young, up became down, past became future, minutes became days, small became large and inanimate objects became living creatures.

At one moment, I was clinging on to a stone desperately trying to base my whole identity on this stone because it remained a stone and I recognised it. To do this I would think something like: "I know stones and this is a stone, this stone still exists and stones are real, so I'm real". I was trying to define myself in some way amongst all of the fluctuating mental and physical forms. Then the stone would dissolve and loose its qualities as a separate object so I could no longer use it as the basis for my existence. I also lost my sensation of personal volition over anything specific that was happening, instead there was a force of volition over everything that was happening, and I felt more aligned with this force the more I lost myself into the experience. Without the sensation of personal free will then the feeling of being anything in particular faded and my boundaries became nebulous.

Eventually I could not fight any longer and my subjective experience melted away and there was a new reality where "I", as I had previously experience myself, was gone. My perception as a separate observer had ceased and only an indescribable state of non-local flowing awareness and forms remained. And this is how it continued for an infinite or instantaneous amount of time. But then, in one moment, I started to feel the sense of myself reforming again. This huge nebulous flow of forms within awareness started to differentiate into myself and my environment again. The location of my perception started to return to a distinguishable place in time and space. The feeling of personal free will over myself came back and it was a blissful feeling. When I regained my ability to construct "my own" thoughts again then the first thing I thought was: "I'm going to be me again" and I was filled with gratitude. As the room came back into recognisable existence around me, my eyes were closed but I could feel that I was lying somewhere on the wooden floor. I had no desire to open my eyes. I didn't need to. I was me again. I was blissfully relieved and grateful but not because I was alive. I was relieved because my death, as I had previously "known" it, and been terrified of when I thought I was dying, was now revealed to me as an illusion.

I had just experienced my death and rebirth. Death had not been the ending of me, as I feared, but the transition into an infinite flow of phenomena and then into another birth of myself, coming back into myself, returning to my limited view but with a deeper insight into reality, and knowledge of a spiritually enlightened perspective. Just as a peak and a valley are two parts of one continuous mountain so life and death are two parts of continuous existence within a continuous universe. I had experienced my subjective consciousness being born all over again, growing from the life all around me. I experienced that what I really am is not the subjective consciousness that I label as myself but I am pure infinite life. I experienced that I am not alive as a transient individual but I am life/nature/the universe itself experiencing a particular pattern within itself. This experience was not a new experience, instead it was an experience of a deep remembering of my true nature from before I was "hypnotised" by the illusion of the self.

The medicine of awakening

The beneficial effects of ayahuasca on mental illnesses including depression and addiction are well-known and documented. The amount of anecdotal evidence for these effects is vast - including reviews of ayahuasca retreats on impartial travel websites like TripAdvisor. A quick search online reveals thousands of in-depth anecdotal descriptions of beneficial ayahuasca experiences. There is also scientific research into these benefits including research publications in the journal of psychopharmacology. One of these publications is titled:

> *'Sub-acute and long-term effects of ayahuasca on affect and cognitive thinking style and their association with ego dissolution'*

Within the results of this publication it states:

> *"depression and stress significantly decreased after the ayahuasca ceremony and these changes persisted for 4 weeks...Changes in affect, satisfaction with life, and mindfulness were significantly correlated to the level of ego dissolution experienced during the ayahuasca ceremony."*

There's another paper titled:

> *'Rapid antidepressant effects of the psychedelic ayahuasca in treatment-resistant depression: a randomized placebo-controlled trial'*

Within the results of this publication it states:

"We observed significant antidepressant effects of ayahuasca when compared with placebo at all-time points."

It states that the more acutely the subject experiences the dissolution of the ego the more they show improvements regarding their mental health disorders. This is because during the process of ego-death and rebirth we experience the death of our individual self, including our ego-story, and the re-establishing of our sense of self again as it returns. As a result, we experience our ego-identity and story, not as a fixed and absolute reality, but as a set of imagined narratives that we identify with to generate our sense of self. When we experience that the defining features of our sense of self are based on the process of identification with imaginary stories, the possibility of changing ourselves (i.e. our story) becomes possible. Our personas, including our character traits, habits and desires etc. can become a fluid and flexible process. Just like when Jim Carrey experienced that the sense he had of himself as Jim Carrey was a fictional character that he was presenting to the world.

For example, a person who identifies with the story "I am depressed" or "I am a smoker" has now experienced that these stories are the basis for their illusory existence. Therefore, they become free to re-imagine their story from a sea of infinite possible stories. A depressed person can now identify as happy without feeling like their actual existence is under threat because it's only the illusion of the self that is being re-imagined. That is to say that conscious awareness itself always remains, however, it is the thoughts, sense perceptions and emotions within that conscious awareness that we are changing when we re-imagine our ego-identity. Once we have experienced our fundamental continuous oneness with the flow of all phenomena then our identification to a story is no longer immutable or dogmatic. An alcoholic can become sober or a shy person can become confident.

An example of someone who was able to re-imagine their ego-story is the Vietnamese Mahayana Buddhist monk: Thích Quảng Đức. He burned himself to death in protest against the south Vietnamese government in 1963 and remained calm, peaceful and silent while he was burning alive. The photographer Malcolm W. Browne, who took the iconic picture of him burning, said in an interview in 2012:

> *"I don't know exactly when he died because you couldn't tell from his features or voice or anything. He never yelled out in pain. His face seemed to remain fairly calm until it was so blackened by the flames that you couldn't make it out anymore."*

We have evolved to have an ego-story where damage to our body is undesirable and because the sensation of damaging our body is pain, therefore, pain is experienced as undesirable. Therefore, we suffer from the sensation of pain. Thích Quảng Đức reversed this fundamental human desire and imagined a new story that was not restricted by his biological conditioning. He wanted to damage his body because it was the act of damaging his body, and sacrificing his life, that he wanted people to see. He changed his story to desire the burning of his body, therefore, he didn't suffer, as we would suffer, from the pain, as is evident by his calm demeanour in the picture. This demonstrates his mastery over his subjective experience. I believe that he consciously achieved this capacity to not suffer by reaching spiritually enlightened conscious awareness. But whether or not he achieved it consciously or unconsciously, the fact is that he no longer suffered from pain in a way that a person suffers from pain who identifies with the ego-story that has been condition by their biology. Again, this is encapsulated in the line that Shakespeare wrote:

"There's nothing either good or bad but thinking makes it so"

In the language of continuous monism: there is nothing either desirable or undesirable but identification with a particular ego-story makes it so.

Hidden fictions

British comedian Simon Amstel has written a book called 'help' in which he documents his participation in several ayahuasca ceremonies. During one ceremony, he explains how he experienced himself as a baby in his mother's womb, and then in a push chair looking at his mother as she was crying. He then heard the voice of his mother and the voice of ayahuasca say: "You couldn't have done anything. You couldn't even crawl". This revealed to him how he had been constructing his ego-story. He now understood that the things he had been trying to achieve throughout his life were an attempt to stop his mother from crying in this hidden memory. This was the cause of his depression. His conditioned narrative was: "If I do the right things with my life, i.e. become a really funny and successful comedian, then my mother will stop crying". It was an unconscious trauma response. Obviously, no matter how successful he became as a stand-up comedian he could never stop his mother crying because the story of his mother crying was a hidden memory in his subconscious. He had gone through a lot of therapy to try and understand why he was so unhappy but it was ayahuasca that expanded his awareness to experience the cause of his depression. So, as a result of this realisation he was able to change his ego-story and his suffering stopped. He no longer needed to identify with this narrative to create his sense of self. He was free to have an alternative story.

Another reason why ayahuasca, and many other spiritual practices are successful at healing traumatic ego-stories is because ego-stories are often created on the preverbal or nonverbal level, just like the example of Simon Amstel's crying mother. This means that, talking about our traumatic stories using verbal linguistic and psychoanalytical therapy won't change our identification with an ego-story that was created on the preverbal or nonverbal level. And actually, talking may reinforce and further entrench our dogmatic identification with a subconscious ego-story. However, as we experience our true nature as the continuous universe during spiritual practice then the fictions of our ego-stories are revealed to us which gives us the freedom to change our identification with them.

A metaphor in a metaphor

There are other psychedelic drugs that have similar medicinal properties to ayahuasca. There is a research publication in the journal of psychopharmacology titled:

'Antidepressive, anxiolytic, and antiaddictive effects of

ayahuasca, psilocybin and lysergic acid diethylamide (LSD): a systematic review of clinical trials published in the last 25 years'

Within the results of this research it states:

"The reported results consistently show that ayahuasca, psilocybin, and LSD have anxiolytic, antidepressive, and antiaddictive properties."

More positive mental health benefits have been discovered in another research publication, in the same journal, regarding psilocybin in combination with spiritual practices which is titled:

'Psilocybin-occasioned mystical-type experience in combination with meditation and other spiritual practices produces enduring positive changes in psychological functioning and in trait measures of prosocial attitudes and behaviours.'

Another publication regarding psilocybin, also in the journal of psychopharmacology, expresses positive results, and is titled:

'Psilocybin produces substantial and sustained decreases in depression and anxiety in patients with life-threatening cancer: A randomized double-blind trial.'

I will now describe one of my own experiences under the effects of LSD when I experienced ego dissolution. In some aspects, it was similar to the ayahuasca experience and in some ways, it was very different. During this experience, what I can best describe as the metaphor of what I took to be my personality and body dissolved, and whatever "I" was now floated outwards to become indistinguishable from all other forms of life around me. I became the trees but I was also observing the trees at the same time. The trees themselves had no fixed state or form and they constantly transmuted into many other creatures, landscapes and places in time and space. These multitude of flowing forms fluttered in and out of existence like flames where each flicker was a new living creature. Everything also became pure geometric shapes from which the entire complexity of organic life seemed to emanate and recede simultaneously. The world was being born and dying in every moment as the processes of creation and destruction were oscillating from one to the other. Trees and plants seamlessly lived their entire life span in full and decayed into oblivion without there being any distinction between the two processes. It was the dissolution of duality. This experience of being continuous with the totality of nature came in waves. Every time that I regained my sense of self then the experience of myself, as a separate entity, disconnected from my environment, was so obviously an illusion to me that I laughed so hard that I cried. I said to my friend: "I am a metaphor of myself and you are a metaphor of yourself in a metaphor of this place". I will describe exactly what I meant by this. Metaphors are a beautiful and useful way of describing reality. Contemplate this metaphor:

'The horse is a roaring steam train'.

This metaphor gives us a creative description and depiction of the horse in our imagination. From this metaphor, we can clearly understand that the horse is a heavy, strong, powerful, fast and magnificent beast to behold. But, even though the metaphor gives us all of this information about the reality of the horse, we are not under the illusion that the horse is actually a steam train. If we believed that the horse was actually a steam train then we would be making a misconstrued interpretation of the actual reality of the horse. In the same way, if we believe in the reality of ourselves as a separate individual then we are believing in a metaphor of ourselves. If we believe that we are a separate fragmented individual, with personal free will, living within a story with a past and a future within a universe of many fragmented parts, then we are believing in the illusion of a metaphorical description and depiction of reality that only exists within our imagination. Our individual sense of self and our ego-stories are useful ways to represent reality because they edit the universe into useful information but that information is not the same as actual reality. Just as the steam train does not actually represent the horse. While under the effects of LSD I had experienced that it is our normal everyday conscious perception that blocks our experience of a reality beyond the metaphor of ourselves.

In a talk called 'My Stroke of Insight' given by neuroanatomist Jill Bolte Taylor, she describes having a stroke and losing the function of the left hemisphere of her brain. Here she describes how our left-brain hemisphere creates our ego-stories and the illusion of our individual self out of the flow of the continuous universe, she says:

> *"Our left hemisphere is all about the past and it's all about the future. Our left hemisphere is designed to take the enormous collage of the present moment and start picking out details...It then categorises and organises all that information, associates*

it with everything in the past that we've ever learned and projects into the future all of our possibilities. Our left hemisphere thinks in language...It's that little voice that says to me "I am". And as soon as my left hemisphere says to me "I am" I become separate, single, solid individual - separate from the energy flow around me. And separate from you."

Therefore, when she lost the function of the left hemisphere of her brain she experienced ego-dissolution and oneness with the continuous universe. She explains how, when she was on an exercise machine having a stroke, her localised spatial perception and personal free will perception dissolved:

"...my consciousness had shifted away from my normal perception of reality where I'm the person on the machine having the experience, to some esoteric space where I'm witnessing myself having this experience."

She then describes her experience of spiritually enlightened consciousness and being one with the continuous universe when the left hemisphere of her brain switched off:

"I realise that I can no longer define the boundaries of my body. I can't define where I begin and where I end, because the atoms and molecules of my arm blended with the atoms and molecules of the wall...I was immediately captivated by the magnificence

of the energy around me. And because I could no longer identify the boundaries of my body I felt at one with all of the energy that was... I felt enormous and expansive, like a genie just liberated from her bottle and my spirit soared free, like a great whale souring through a silent sea of euphoria.... I found nirvana...We are the life force power of the universe. I am the life-force power of the 50 trillion beautiful molecular geniuses that make up my form at one with all that is."

Next, she describes the experience of the fragmented universe when she speaks from the perspective of the left hemisphere of her brain (i.e. normal everyday conscious perception):

"I become a single individual. A solid. Separate from the flow. Separate from you. I am Dr Jill Bolte Taylor. Intellectual. Neuroanatomist."

More awake in a dream

Why do we sleep? In terms of our evolution, it seems that sleeping for eight hours every day would be a huge disadvantage for our survival. We could achieve so much more if we didn't sleep. During sleep, early homo sapiens would have been vulnerable to predators. Sleep is a vast amount of time that we could have used for things like finding food and rearing offspring. Therefore, the fact that we do sleep for one third of our lives tells us that is must serve an incredibly vital function for our survival, but what is it?

There are physically regenerative processes that occur during sleep. However, scientists agree that there must be many more essential processes that benefit our physiology and psychology but we just don't know what they are. There are theories regarding the purposes of sleep but the question of why we sleep still mostly remains a mystery. However, there is evidence to suggest that the purpose of sleeping and dreaming is to achieve ego-dissolution and spiritually enlightened states of consciousness within our everyday lives.

When we sleep we lose our subjective awareness and all that seems to remain for us is nothingness. Our sense of time becomes meaningless, which is evident because when we wake then we don't know how much time has passed. We seem to have no conscious sensations apart from when we dream. Our perception, as a conscious individual, melts away into a void. Contemplate this period of black emptiness that we seem to experience during sleep. Compare this sensation to what we imagine death to be like. Compare it to the experience of "nonexistence" from before we were born and we have to admit that it's the same. We fear death because we believe we will disappear and stop experiencing anything anymore, but every night we experience the same sensation as death and we accept it, and even enjoy it. So, why don't we fear sleep? We don't fear sleep because we know that we will wake up again and we will become ourselves again. However, this is just our faith and belief that we will regain consciousness again when we wake up in the morning. The fact remains that we accept this literal death-like oblivion of our individual consciousness every night when we fall asleep, followed by our rebirth every morning when we wake up. Waking and sleeping is a perfect analogy for life and death. It is the fluctuation of consciousness, just as a wave fluctuates between the peak and dip of the wave, consciousness fluctuates between awake and asleep, alive and dead, conscious and unconscious. Although each fluctuation in consciousness represents one individual perceiver, each individual perceiver is a fluctuation within one continuous process, within one united sea of consciousness.

Where are we when we are asleep? Where is our awareness when it disappears when we are unconscious? Our awareness didn't go anywhere because it's not our awareness. Meaning that our awareness is not confined to our normal everyday conscious perception as an individual perceiver. We know this because while we are asleep, if there is a loud noise then we will wake up, because, although we are not consciously aware of the noise, awareness of the noise within consciousness itself still exists because it still wakes us up. This example illustrates that consciousness is more expansive, and includes much more phenomena than we experience during normal everyday conscious perception. Awareness is also not confined to our brain. Consciousness is created by all brains within one continuous uninterrupted process which constitutes the universe. The illusion of a separate fragmented individual point of awareness is a misconstrued interpretation of our experience of reality. We know this because all awareness and all brains are the result of the single process of the total entangled universe. The experience of ourselves, as a separate conscious individual, is an illusory interpretation of ourselves, generated by the pattern of the whole universe flowing through the pattern of our individual nervous system.

When we sleep, the mind phenomena that make up our ego-identity dissolve because we are unconscious and, consequently, no longer experiencing normal everyday conscious perception. Therefore, we become connected to primary reality, beyond the illusion of the fragmented universe, so we can experience any possible reality within our dreams. Our dreams free us from the limited, fixed and misconstrued imagination of ourselves as a separate individual. Therefore, when we dream, we are experiencing a spiritually enlightened perspective of our internal world.

When we dream, we become open to true inspiration. New ideas, new ways of thinking, new concepts and new ways of defining ourselves appear that can't be experienced during normal everyday conscious awareness. Therefore, in order to evolve new ideas in new and original ways, we must experience dreams. This is why they play a vital role in our lives.

The psychedelic experience is very similar to the dream experience, except that the psychedelic experience includes the flow of information from the physical world that we absorb though our senses, whereas, the dream experience does not, because we are asleep. Our dream reality is purely created from our internal world of transpersonal free will in relationship with our imagination and our emotions. However, both dreams and psychedelic experiences are similar because they both facilitate our ego-dissolution. Sleep does this by literally "shutting down" our individual conscious awareness and therefore opening our awareness to an unbounded flow of thoughts, memories and emotions within consciousness itself. We know that our sense of personal free will dissolves in our dreams because we become the witness of our own actions. The memories of our waking life can be re-imagined and re-written so that all possible scenarios become plausible within an infinite potential of dream realities.

We have evolved to experience dreams because they are essential for our survival. For any "real" thinking to occur we need to spend time dreaming because dreams untether our awareness and our imagination from the constraints of our ego-identity. Dreams can liberate us from the ego-stories that we dogmatically identify with during our waking life. Therefore, our dreams change the way that we think and feel about the world by developing our thoughts and ideas beyond what we already know. This is also a way for us to overcome traumatic memories that we have written into our ego-story by re-imagining our past in our dreams and, therefore, releasing ourselves from the suffering that our traumatic memories cause for us. That is why this deeply inspirational, creative and spiritually enlightened perspective, free from the dogmatic imagination of ourselves, is naturally part of our lives every time we sleep.

Think about your own life. How many times have you been looking for an answer that seemed impossibly out of reach? But, after you have slept, and awoke in the morning, then the answer came to you spontaneously and with no effort? It is only when we are dreaming, meditating, or in flow state (i.e. experiencing spiritually enlightened conscious perception) that we are actually connected to original patterns of thought that are more than maintaining a rigid illusion of ourselves.

The list of people who have been inspired by dreams is endless. Here are a few famous examples from the realm of science:

The Double Helix structure of DNA:

Nobel laureate James Watson, co-discoverer of the structure of DNA, reported seeing the double helix image for the DNA chain through his dream of a spiral staircase.

The Structure of the atom:

Neils Bohr won the Nobel prize in physics in 1922 for his discovery of the structure of the atom. He recalled that the electrons revolving around the nucleus, like the solar system, came to him in a dream.

The Periodic table:

"I saw in a dream a table where all elements fell into place as required. Awakening, I immediately wrote it down on a piece of paper, only in one place did a correction later seem necessary."

— Dmitri Mendeleev (Russian Chemist), as quoted by Inostrantzev

Descartes' new science:

Descartes claimed that the dreams that he had on November 10th, 1619, revealed to him the basis of a new philosophy: the scientific method.

Carl Jung encapsulates this notion of dreams connecting us to something far beyond our ego-consciousness and to deeper, more fundamental truths when he wrote:

"Dreams are impartial, spontaneous products of the unconscious psyche, outside the control of the will. They are pure nature; they show us the unvarnished, natural truth, and are therefore fitted, as nothing else is, to give us back an attitude that accords with our basic human nature when our consciousness has strayed too far from its foundations and run into an impasse...To concern ourselves with dreams is a way of reflecting on ourselves – a way of self-reflection...It is not our ego-consciousness reflecting on itself; rather it turns its attention to the objective actuality of the dream as a communication or message from the unconscious, unitary soul of humanity"

The trickster

"...that the experience you are having that you call ordinary everyday consciousness - pretending you're not it - that experience is exactly the same thing as "IT". There's no difference at all. And when you find that out, you laugh yourself silly. That's the great discovery." - Alan Watts

"Tragedy turns into comedy when you watch your own drama and realising it as a mind-created fiction designed to create you a sense of identity." - Eckhart Tolle

There are many theories of humour but they can be differentiated into two main categories. The first broad category of humour and laughter is the laughter we experience as a bonding tool and a social mechanism to form the structures of hierarchal relationships between individuals and groups in a society. For example, a dominant individual or bully laughs at an outsider, and the allies of the bully laugh to show their allegiance to the bully and the others in group. For example, in Britain, one type of traditional racist joke which elicits this type of laughter consist of an English man, an Irish man and a Scottish man. The Irish man is portrayed as stupid. These jokes are a mechanism to inforce identification with an ego-story in which the English and the Scottish are more superior and intelligent than the Irish. By laughing at the Irish man, it establishes a hierarchy between the groups and bonds the individuals in the groups who are laughing. There is more to this first type of laughter which I won't go into but these two quotes get to the essence of this humour. In a published paper called 'Comedy and critical thought: Laughter as resistance' it states:

> *"Teenagers mobilise humour against the misfit, the nerd, the overweight, the already-outcast."*

It states in the BBC Science Focus Magazine:

> *"We use laughter to show others that we're being playful and non-threatening, and this serves to make and maintain social bonds."*

The other type of laughter is a reflexive physical manifestation of an experience of spiritually enlightened consciousness. We have been describing this type of humour for thousands of years in the form of stories involving the traditional archetypal character of 'the trickster'. The trickster is a character which has its origins within mythology, folklore and religion, and is best summarised by these quotes from the scholar Lewis Hyde in his book titled: 'Trickster Makes this World':

> *"...[Tricksters] violate principles of social and natural order, playfully disrupting normal life and then re-establishing it on a new basis."*

> *"Trickster isn't a run-of-the-mill liar and thief. When he lies and*

steals, it isn't so much to get away with something or get rich as to disturb the established categories of truth and property and, by so doing, open the road to possible new worlds."

"Trickster is at one and the same time creator and destroyer, giver and negator, he who dupes others and who is always duped himself... He knows neither good nor evil yet he is responsible for both. He possesses no value, moral or social... yet through his actions all values come into being"

The laughter and humour of the trickster manifests as a result of one reality or story being subverted, juxtaposed, replaced or contradicted by another reality or story. These two or more realities, which are incongruous, exist simultaneously within the comedic devise. This process reveals the illusory nature of all of our ego-stories which results in us experiencing ego dissolution which manifests as a euphoric feeling and laughter. When our ego dissolves, so does the effort and the worry caused by our constant striving for our desired future. Therefore, when we experience this type of laughter, we are liberated from the burden of our existence which feels hilarious because all of a sudden, our ego-identity doesn't matter anymore, actually, nothing in our life matters as we thought it did.

An example of this is 'misdirection' which occurs when the setup of the joke makes the audience create one reality in their imaginations with a desired and predicted future in the form of a punchline. But the actual punchline that is delivered subverts the reality that has already been constructed in the imagination of the audience. The joke reveals how our reality is a construction in our imaginations and exposes our identities as fictions. Here is an example of a joke by Anthony Jeselnik containing misdirection:

"Yeah, we're not together anymore. She's got a new boyfriend now. They just moved in together. And I've heard rumors that he is abusive, which makes me want to go over there with a baseball bat. And then blame it on her boyfriend."

The first reality is a man who is upset that his ex-girlfriend is in an abusive relationship. The second is a man who still hates his ex-girlfriend so much that he wishes her harm. Here is another one, this time by Sarah Silverman:

"Once I was with two men in one night. But I could never do it again—I could hardly walk afterward. Two dinners? That's a lot of food."

One reality is a woman who had sex twice in one night which made it hard for her to walk, and another reality is a woman who had two dinner dates and ate so much that it was hard to walk. The second reality subverts our expectations of the first. In the moment that we are surprised by the flip between the two realities we experience freedom from all realities and stories. Both stories are illusory and Silverman is playing with reality itself. We feel relief because our stories and, therefore, our perceived reality is an illusion, and so we laugh. This type of humour has been encapsulated by many people and here are some examples:

"a great joke creates a beautiful expectation and then creatively subverts it" – Reggie Watts - Comedian

"Humour takes what we know to be true and flips it on its head." - Judd Apatow – comedian

"Comedic tropes...revel in the play between reality, intentionality, and meaning: irony, sarcasm, exaggeration, slapstick...humour surprises and undercuts" – Kennan Ferguson – political theorist and writer

A story-telling observational comedian finds incongruities by subverting narratives that the majority of us identify with. This means that the narratives they subvert have become accepted and unchallenged by most of us. Here is a story by comedian Joe Rogan which subverts the narrative of vegan people as animal lovers:

"We all have friends that are vegans who also have cats and you go over to their house and you're like:

"So why are you vegan again?"

"I just don't think that it's our right to decide that an animal should live or die"

Then they open up a fat can of murder and give it to that little...psychopath that they live with...If you're a vegan with a pet cat, that's like being a doctor with a pet vampire."

The story/reality of an animal loving vegan can't exist simultaneously with the story/reality of a person with a pet predatory carnivore. We base our existence on these stories and they can't be real. This type of humour is also illustrated in the 'ontic-epistemic theory of humour' which was proposed by Peter Marteinson in 2006 and is summarised like this:

"laughter is a reaction to a cognitive impasse, a momentary epistemological difficulty, in which the subject perceives that social being itself suddenly appears no longer to be real in any factual or normative sense."

From the perspective of normal everyday consciousness, having our ego-story contradicted in an argument makes us suffer because we feel that our ego-identity is under threat from our opponent's conflicting story. This creates suffering as we don't want to let go of our stories because they are the bases for our existence. Therefore, we retaliate and defend our ego-story by making a counter argument to oppose their story. In the same way, a person who identifies dogmatically with their ego-story might experience the two realities of the trickster as an argument against their ego-story. They will then find the joke offensive and maybe even as an abomination. They may fear comedians as dangerous, immoral and provocative because they destabilise their dogmatic reality. Using the example of Joe Rogan's vegan joke, a person who dogmatically identifies with the ego-story of vegans as animal lovers may be offended by the joke as a personal attack on their ego-identity and not as freedom from the illusion of it. We see this trait within tyrannical world leaders who have an inability to laugh at the trickster. This includes people who identify so dogmatically with their ego-story they want to impose their illusory future reality on everyone.

When our ego-story is subverted and exposed as an illusion in a creative, joyful and playful way by the trickster then we can feel blissful liberation from identification with it. This liberation is expressed as a physical release of the tension in the form of laughter, as we are, for that moment, free of the burden of maintaining the illusion of ourselves.

Here are some examples of comedic devices which consist of two or more contradictory and incongruous realities:

Irony and sarcasm – 'The expression of one's meaning by using language that normally signifies the opposite. Or, a state of affairs or an event that seems deliberately contrary to what one expects.'

Double entendre – 'A word or phrase open to two interpretations, one of which is usually risqué or indecent.'

Juxtaposition – 'the fact of two things being seen or placed close together with contrasting effect. When the comparison is unexpected, it creates irony.'

Pun – 'A pun consists of a deliberate confusion of similar words or phrases for humorous effect. A pun can rely on the assumed equivalency of multiple similar words (homonymy), of different shades of meaning of one word (polysemy), or of a literal meaning with a metaphor.'

The comedian Russell Brand encapsulates the idea of the humour of the trickster on a podcast in 2019 when he said:

"Comedy presents you quite quickly with two opposing ideas and there is the sudden revelation of the truth behind the idea and relief is experienced...All humour is underwritten by our mutual awareness that the reality we are living in is not the reality. It's not real. We know this on some level - that people are going: "You can't park there" and "This is the way we do things in this family" and "This is what makes this country great." And underneath It, somewhere deep within you is the awareness that none of this is real, that it's bullshit, that it's absurd, that it's all going to fall away. And through comedy you can, just for a moment, touch that, make a connection with that awareness and it lights up like any circuit. And the laughter is the consequence of that temporary illumination, of that temporary connection."

The stand-up comedian Bill Hicks was roleplaying the part of a serious news reporter within his routine when he said:

"Today a young man on acid realised that all matter is merely energy condensed to a slow vibration, that we are all one

consciousness experiencing itself subjectively, there is no such thing as death, life is only a dream, and we are the imagination of ourselves. Here's Tom with the weather."

Chapter Seven: Hypothesis

Where do we exist?

We exist within three-dimensional space. These dimensions of space are a fundamental feature of the experience of our local point of awareness. Having this perception of space allows us to navigate ourselves through a three-dimensional landscape and differentiate our location from other locations in space. The three dimensions of space are up-down, left-right and forward-back or width, depth and length.

There are many models within theoretical physics which contain mathematical evidence that suggests that the universe has many more dimensions of space than three. However, during normal everyday conscious perception we can't experience these other dimensions through our senses, or measure them with any of our current measuring devises. These theories include: string theory, M-theory and matrix theory. Could there be other conscious creatures within the universe that experience more dimensions of space than we do? This may seem like a fanciful question to ask at first glance, but given that we know that the reality that we experience during our normal everyday lives is not as it seems, then answering this question could be critical in understanding what is actually real. If these creatures exist then they would experience a very different subjective universe from the one that we experience. If these creatures were all around us in the universe but living within different dimensions of space then how would we know that they are here? How would we be able to interact with them at all?

There is an analogy that illustrates what this might be like. Imagine that there is another creature in the universe that experiences fewer dimensions than we do. They are called ‘Flat Landers’ because, in their world, they do not experience the vertical/up-down dimension of space. This concept of a ‘Flatland’ was created by the author Edwin Abbott Abbott in his 1884 novella ‘Flatland: A Romance of Many Dimensions’. Try to imagine how these Flat Landers would see us. They are completely flat and have no height what so ever. When we pass through their horizontal level of perception they would only see a cross section of our body – a flat slice of our organism. When we move up or down far enough then we would move beyond their horizontal level of perception and we would disappear from their universe of experience. As we pass through their horizontal level of perception they would experience a very restricted view of us. We would remain a total mystery to them. They wouldn’t be able to experience what we are or understand what was entering their world and disappearing again. If we could find a way of communicating with them then how would we describe what up and down is like. We simply couldn’t do it. Up only exists in opposition to down within our experience of the universe. In the same way that we can’t describe the colour blue to someone who has always been blind.

But what if a Flat Lander ingested a drug like ayahuasca and the psychedelic substance could change their nervous system so that the individual could then experience the dimensions of up and down. Then they could experience us and meet us and we could show them what our perception of a universe with three dimensions looks like. Eventually the drug would wear off and they would go back to being a creature that only experiences two spatial dimensions again. How would this individual describe us to the other Flat Landers? What would the other Flat Landers think of them? Maybe the others would think that they are crazy because they were trying to describe something that is impossible to describe. Maybe they would be told that they were just hallucinating the extra dimension of space because they were on drugs and what they experienced wasn't real.

Seeing the unseen

Would it be possible for us to experience other conscious beings that live alongside us but within different dimensions of space just like in the example of the flat landers? This would mean that we can't see them from the perspective of our normal everyday conscious experience.

In order for these other conscious entities to exist within more dimensions it would require there to be a lot more universe than we have ever been able to perceive or measure. However, scientists have discovered that 95% of the universe is unmeasurable by any of our current instruments and is made of something totally undetected by humans. We simply have no idea what the majority of the universe consists of. Physicists have labelled this stuff 'dark matter' and 'dark energy'. There are many experiments that show us that dark matter and dark energy exist. We can measure dark matter and dark energy indirectly but not directly. Here is one example of an experiment that allows us to indirectly know that we can't see what most of the universe is composed of.

We can measure how much matter there is in space because matter generates gravity. The more matter there is then the more gravity is produced. Gravity bends light and so, the amount that light bends as it travels through space is proportional to the amount of matter that exists. When scientists measure the curvature of light travelling through the universe they have discovered that there is much more matter than we can observe. They know this because the light is curving much more than it would from only the matter that we can measure directly. However, we can't see this extra matter, or know what it's made from, or know anything about it, we just know that it is there. But we do know that dark energy and dark matter must be all around us all of the time. In exactly the same way that the Flat Landers would see a cross section of us in their reality but would not see what we actually consist of. So, we know that there is a lot more of the universe all around us than we can perceive. On Nasa's website (nasa.gov) it states:

> *"It turns out that roughly 68% of the universe is dark energy. Dark matter makes up about 27%. The rest - everything on Earth, everything ever observed with all of our instruments, all normal matter - adds up to less than 5% of the universe."*

Crossing boundaries of perception

Almost every time a person drinks ayahuasca or smokes DMT (i.e. the active ingredient in ayahuasca) they come into contact with an intelligent being or beings. This being is commonly referred to as 'mother ayahuasca' or, if there is more than one entity then they are often referred to as 'machine elves'. The name 'machine elves' was coined by the late ethnobotanist, writer and philosopher Terence McKenna. This experience of interacting with autonomous and intelligent entities does not only occur in a few rare cases, it is an extremely consistent effect of ingesting tryptamines such as DMT.

I am not claiming that these lifeforms are definitely real, however I am putting forward this hypothesis to demonstrate that they could be. And even if we do discover that they are not real in the same way that we are real, they could still tell us something vital about the nature of the universe or consciousness itself. This is because when we ingest ayahuasca we are no longer confined to the limits of normal everyday conscious awareness. These other dimensions could exist, but we simply don't experience them because the human nervous system constructs our reality from only three dimensions. Ayahuasca could reconfigure our nervous system to generate our subjective reality from more dimensions than three. We could then experience more of the universe than we have ever been able to perceive. Other conscious entities may exist within these other dimensions of space for us to interact with.

Roland Griffiths is a professor in the departments of psychiatry and neurosciences at the Johns Hopkins University School of Medicine. In an interview in 2019 he talked about the findings of a large survey study into the effects of DMT and the reports of the phenomena of interacting with autonomous entities:

> *"It was most often described as a being or guide or spirit. Most people felt like they communicated with that entity, described the predominant emotions that they and the entity experience as love, kindness and joy...They're saying that this entity was more real than everyday waking consciousness. They believe that this entity existed, it continued to exist after the experience*

and profoundly changed their basic conception of reality. We ask them what attributes do they attribute to this being. And the top ones were intelligence, consciousness and benevolence."

Evoking true reality

"We live in a fantasy world, a world of illusion. The great task in life is to find reality." - Iris Murdoch (Writer and philosopher)

To illustrate my hypothesis, imagine a character on a computer game and another character on a different, more complex computer game but both games are on the same computer. The character on the simpler game represents a human and the character on the more complex game represents the other autonomous entity that can be experienced under the effects of DMT. Then imagine that a computer programmer reprograms the software of the two computer games to allow them to be played simultaneously, on the same screen, so that the two characters from the two games can interact. The computer programmer represents DMT which reprograms our nervous system. The two separate characters can now meet and interact within one game, which would be an amalgamation of the two games. The two entities were always occupying the same space (i.e. the same computer) but they could never interact with each other before because they existed in different digital dimensions (i.e. different computer games). Ayahuasca is like a computer programmer who can reprogram our nervous system to experience a reality with more dimensions. In primary reality, we were never separate from these other entities because we are continuous with them as we are all continuous with one universe.

My own interaction with another seemingly conscious entity came during my third and fourth ayahuasca ceremonies. I have to state once again how inadequate language is at capturing the true reality of this experience but it's all we have. Unlike the experience of the ceremony I previously described, these ceremonies did not cause any suffering for me as a result my ego dissolution. They were peaceful and at times, euphoric. At the beginning of the ceremony I experienced complex visual and audio sensations that were a complex geometric multiplicity of vibrating patterns connected to the nature around me. Then there came a moment, during the climax of the experience, when these noises and visuals subsided and in the middle of this calm, an autonomous entity emerged from the darkness. Its head was a balloon of pure white glowing light that floated and trembled a few feet away from me. From the base of its head hung a neck of ribbon like tendrils that were also luminous. They hung down, quivering and trailing behind it like the long tentacles of a jellyfish. Its eyes had no features such as pupils but instead they consisted of multi-coloured streaks of light that flickered as it gazed at me. It was observing me intently and intensely. As it approached, it's luminous rainbow eyes danced and its whole form vibrated and buzzed. It moved closer and stopped a few centimetres away from my face. Its vibrations resonated through my body and it felt like the energy from these vibrations were being absorbed into the central core of my chest. This process made me feel physically and emotionally warm and relaxed. I accept that any of my interpretations of its intentions and motives are conjecture based purely on our physical interaction. However, I feel it is worth describing my interpretations of its intentions because my experience matches so many descriptions that have been given by other people who have ingested tryptamines. This entity never seemed threatening. It looked curious and seemed to know much more about what was happening than I did. During this ceremony (ceremony number three), it merely introduced itself to me, but during the next ceremony, the same entity returned in exactly the same way, only this time it was not as bright. During the fourth ceremony, after it approached, it travelled into my body through my chest. It then moved around inside my body, vibrating through each part of me, and the vibrations felt warm and healing. It seemed to have a job to do like a doctor and was inspecting my body, maybe looking for problems to fix. I felt as though it knew what it was doing. The internal vibrating presence of this entity stayed with me, and if I focus then I can still vaguely feel its presence today.

The psychiatrist and psychedelic researcher Stanislav Grof wrote this about the psychedelic peak experience which matches the visual attributes of the creature that I encountered:

> *"in most instances, this experience is accompanied by visions of brilliant white or golden light, rainbow spectra or elaborate designs resembling peacock feathers."*

In an online video called 'Terrance McKenna describes DMT trip', he describes a composite of forty DMT trips and describes all of the commonalities between them. One of the commonalities is that they met multiple intelligent entities. He talks about how they went through a membrane to meet these beings and he says: "they are like jewelled self-dribbling basket balls". He points out that by trying to describe them with language we are "downloading it into a lower dimension". He goes on:

"there are many of them and they come pounding towards you and they vibrate but then they do a very disconcerting thing. They jump into your body and they jump back out again"

Many of the features of the DMT trip that he describes are similar to my own and many are different but these differences are still common features of the experiences of the people that he surveyed. For example, he goes on to describe how these entities sing impossible objects into existence which he calls "celestial toys" and those objects can sing other objects into being.

These types of psychedelic experiences could give us great insights into the unknown parts of the universe and possibly answer many unanswered questions about reality if we were to truly study them. Interestingly, there is also many similarities between these psychedelic experiences and those described in naturally occurring so-called "God encounters" as is detailed in a publication titled:

'Survey of subjective "God encounter experiences": Comparisons among naturally occurring experiences and those occasioned by the classic psychedelics psilocybin, LSD, ayahuasca, or DMT'

It's also worth observing the similarities that have been discovered between these descriptions and those of near-death experiences and claims of so-called "alien abductions".

We could try and rule out this hypothesis as impossible because of a misconstrued and preconceived belief about the nature of reality. For example, if we believe that the universe is only constituted of unconscious matter (i.e. we follow a materialist physicalist monist belief) then we may argue that any experience under the effects of ayahuasca is not real. Then we may argue that the experience only exists within consciousness and because consciousness doesn't really exist then the experience doesn't reveal anything about the real universe. However, this can't be true because everything that exists, including all matter, only exists within conscious experience. The instruments that we use to measure the matter of the universe (that a materialist physicalist may argue is objective reality) only exist within consciousness. As I described in chapter three - matter creates consciousness and consciousness creates matter in one continuous process. We are made of matter and we are conscious, therefore, matter is not unconscious. The universe is conscious and so the universe is made of consciousness as much as matter because they are one and the same process.

A large portion of the people who ingest ayahuasca experience contact with an autonomous entity or entities. This demonstrates a commonality of experience. This should be considered as empirical evidence for these experiences containing fundamental information about the universe. It is, after all, the constancies in our perceptions and measurements of the universe that allow us to create models of reality.

From a materialist perspective, we may argue that we can't experience more of the universe through our senses because the human senses are very limited. For example, the human eye can only perceive a small bandwidth of the electromagnetic spectrum (i.e. visible light). We may argue that this means that we can't sense anything outside of the limitation of our sense organs. This is correct, but I'm going to argue that our physical mechanisms can be liberated from our illusion of the fragmented universe. Moreover, that liberation may also allow us to experience the unknown dark matter and energy that is all around us but is undetected by our normal everyday conscious experience.

Scientists are looking for dark matter and dark energy that they know is there but they can't measure directly. They have built machines to try and detect and measure dark matter but so far, they have not found any of it. But even the most complex machines that they can build are very simplistic in comparison with the complexity of the universe and so these measuring devices have failed. However, we all have access to the most complex and powerful measuring device in the known universe. It is, of course, the human nervous system including the human brain which is the most complex structure in the known universe. What is the human nervous system? It's a measuring device. It measures the universe and constructs a subjective reality by editing the information of the entire flow of the universe that it is also continuous with. The human nervous system is a continuous and entangled part of the universe, through which the universe measures itself and, from those measurements, it evokes itself as a separate subjective individual and as an environment to experience itself within. I'm proposing that our nervous system can fundamentally shift its neurological mechanisms to evoke a new interpretation of reality with more dimensions that we usually experience. Usually, our conscious awareness evokes a separate individual self which looks outwards at a separate environment which it also evokes. But that separation is an illusion and when that illusory boundary between self and environment dissolves then the consciousness of the universe (i.e. we) becomes able to experience more of itself (i.e. ourselves). This is because the illusion of self and other fades and the experience becomes connected to the total flow of information (i.e. the continuous universe) instead of being limited to our usual constructed reality. Within this flow there is dark matter and dark energy. To summarise: we are the whole universe experiencing a particular subjective part of itself and that particular part that we experience can shift by changing the chemistry of our nervous system using a substance like ayahuasca.

This is how it works: Think back to the double slit experiment and what it demonstrated about the true nature of photons of light. It demonstrated that all light photons are really just one continuous wave of light which is 'waving' across all points in time and space simultaneously. Then, when we look through our eyes (i.e. our nervous system), the one wave of light breaks down to be perceived as individual photons of light that appear somewhere in a specific place in space and time within three dimensions of space. However, when we ingest ayahuasca then our nervous systems reconfigure to evoke a universe with more than three dimensions. Therefore, when we have ingested ayahuasca and look at the one continuous wave of light, the wave breaks down into individual photons of light that can now appear anywhere within these new dimensions (i.e. more than three dimensions). That's because these new dimensions have been "opened up" to us by the new configuration of the nervous system which was caused by the absorption of ayahuasca into the system. It wasn't the light or our eyes that fundamentally changed. It was our internal neurological mechanism and brain chemistry which generates our subjective universe within conscious awareness. And that change brought these extra dimensions into the conscious experience of the individual and these autonomous entities (i.e. 'Mother Ayahuasca' or 'Machine Elves') occupy the realm of these other dimensions. I am using photons of light as an example but the double slit experiment has proven that all atoms and particles of matter behave in the same way as light particles (i.e. they are all one wave until they are experienced). Therefore, these other dimensions would be experienced as a full sensory reality by all of our senses and not just our eyes. This hypothesis could be tested by gathering information from these entities and bringing that information back into our normal everyday conscious experience of three dimensions and the validity of that information can be tested.

A similar discovery to this has been scientifically documented with experiments regarding Wim Hof's abilities to trigger his own autonomic nervous system. He achieves this ability by entering a state of deep meditation by getting into very cold water for long periods of time and by using breathing techniques. These methods facilitate a change in his physiology that open up his awareness to encompass his own autonomic systems which he can then control. When he was injected with E-coli bacteria under laboratory conditions he was able to consciously trigger his own autonomic immune response to the infection. It was thought impossible to "reprogram" the human nervous system in this way to achieve awareness/control over these processes but Wim Hof, and many of the people who follow his methods, have proved otherwise. There are many other examples of people who experience reality through altered neurological states that give them a much more expansive conscious awareness than people with a more typical neurological state. For example, the British architectural artist Stephen Wiltshire is an autistic savart. This autistic condition expands his conscious awareness to encompass much more detailed memories of the world. As a result of this ability, he was able to draw the entire cityscape of New York city, in great detail, and with a great degree of accuracy, all from memory. His conscious awareness is much more expansive and includes much more detailed memories of his experiences than anyone who is confined to a typical neurological state of awareness.

I am suggesting a very similar "opening up" of our awareness by tapping deep down into our physiology by altering the chemical configuration of our nervous system. Only, instead of becoming aware of the processes inside our bodies, like Wim Hof does, or becoming aware of much more of our visual memories, like Stephen Wiltshire does, although this could also be a possibility, I'm making the case here that substances such as ayahuasca open up our awareness of other dimensions of space. The shaman in the Peruvian Amazon rain forest have been conducting this experiment for thousands of years. There are thousands of participants that have experienced much more of the universe than people who have remained confined to normal everyday conscious perception. These experiences are happening every day and new discoveries about consciousness and matter are being experienced all the time. However, many of us are choosing to dismiss them because it does not fit in to the current ego-story of mainstream materialist science which many of us dogmatically identify with.

I need to be clear that I am not writing negatively about science. The scientific method has already revealed a vast amount of evidence for spiritually enlightened conscious perception and the continuous universe in the form of quantum mechanics, relativity and all of the discoveries and research that I have cited in this book. The only problem is that in some areas of mainstream scientific materialism there is a dogmatic misconstrued belief that the universe is only unconscious matter. Therefore, the results of these areas of science are being misinterpreted.

We need to start interpreting the results of these experiments from the perspective of primary reality - the perspective that we are atoms looking at atoms. We are the universe evoking itself subjectively. We are simultaneously consciousness and matter and both are as real as the other and can't be separated. Consciousness evokes matter and matter evokes consciousness in a continuous universe. That's continuous monism. Through experiences of psychedelics, meditation, flow and other spiritual practices we can achieve ego-dissolution and reach spiritually enlightened conscious perception. Then our primary reality and fundamental oneness with the totality of phenomena is revealed to us. Richard Feynman wrote:

"out of the cradle
onto dry land
here it is
standing:
atoms with consciousness;
matter with curiosity."

During a lecture Alan Watts states:

"If you awaken from this illusion, and you understand that black implies white, self implies other, life implies death – or shall I say, death implies life – you can feel yourself not as a stranger in the world, not as someone here on sufferance, on probation, not as something that has arrived here by fluke, but you can begin to feel your own existence as absolutely fundamental. What you are basically, deep, deep down, far, far in is simply the fabric and structure of existence itself."

The universe is dissolving its own illusion of separateness. That's what you (i.e. the universe) are doing now by reading this book. The universe is waking itself up to itself like a dream becoming lucid. There is no trying to be something else. Just accept, surrender and be. You are it.

About the Author

Ben Moores is an actor, writer, physical theatre practitioner, educator and truth seeker. He trained in ballet and holds a Masters degree in ensemble theatre. He has been writing plays and creating original theatre for over fifteen years. During this time, as well as training his body and mind he has developed a passion for science, philosophy and spirituality and has read widely within in areas relevant to this book. He has been performing talks on the subject of 'continuous monism' and wishes to continue to do so. To find out more about these talks and how you can attend please find all of the information on his company's website and follow him on Facebook or twitter. Please add a review of the book on Amazon to let him know what you think.

theatreelliptical.co.uk
facebook.com/theatreelliptical
@TElliptical

Acknowledgments

A special thank you to Helen Bazen, Montse Gili, Tikki Emad, Gren Bartley, Elizabeth Lye, Sumit Sarkar, Farhad Emad, and my mum. Thank you for your huge generosity of time, support, encouragement and advice.

Thanks for reading! Please add a short review on Amazon and let me know what you thought!

References

Amstell, S. help (Square Peg. 2017)

Apatow, J. "How to Write a Joke in 7 Easy Steps" Available at https://www.masterclass.com/articles/how-to-write-a-joke-in-7-easy-steps#what-makes-a-good-joke [Last accessed July 2020]

Barbour, J. The End of Time: The Next Revolution in Physics. (Weidenfeld & Nicolson. 1999)

Barbour, J. "The Illusion of Now" Available at **https://iai.tv/video/the-illusion-of-now-is-time-static-or-fluid** [Last accessed July 2020]

Barbour, J. "Time, Space and Being" Available **https://iai.tv/video/time-space-and-being** [Last accessed July 2020]

Beck, E. D. Spiral Dynamics Integral: Learn to Master the Memetic Codes of Human Behavior (Sounds True. 2006)

Binet, A. The Mind and the Brain (Kessinger Publishing. 2010. Originally published in 1905)

Bohm, D. Wholeness and the Implicate Order (Routledge. 1980)

Bohm, D. "The Best Dr. David Bohm Interview" Available at https://www.youtube.com/watch?v=r-jl0zzYgIE&t=2012s [Lasted accessed January 2020]

Bohm, D. "David Bohm speaks about Wholeness and Fragmentation" Available at https://www.youtube.com/watch?v=mDKB7GcHNacc [Lasted accessed January 2020]

Bohm, D. "Interview with David Bohm" Available at https://www.youtube.com/watch?v=Ql66ZglzcO0&t=2140s [Lasted accessed January 2020]

Botton, D. A. "The School Of Life: How To Apply Philosophy To Real Life" Avaliable at https://londonreal.tv/alain-de-botton-the-school-of-life-how-to-apply-philosophy-to-real-life/ [Last accessed April 2020]

Brand, R. "How To Laugh at Reality / Russell Brand" Available at https://www.podbean.com/media/share/dir-pxxwb-5dd94d0 [Last accessed January 2020]

Brook, P. The Empty Space. (New York, NY: Simon &Schuster. 1968)

Browne, W. M. "Malcolm Browne: The Story Behind The Burning Monk" (time.com. 2012) Available at https://time.com/3791176/malcolm-browne-the-story-behind-the-burning-monk/ [Lasted accessed January 2020]

Bryson, B. The Body; A Guide for Participants (Doubleday Canada. 2019)

Bucke, M. R. Cosmic Consciousness: A Study in the Evolution of the Human Mind. (Applewood Books 2000. Originally published in 1901)

Buniy, R.V., & Hsu, S.D.H. (2012). Everything is entangled. Physics Letters B, 718(2): 233-236. doi: 10.1016/j.physletb.2012.09.047

Carpenter, W. B. On the influence of suggestion in modifying and directing muscular movement, independently of volition. (Royal Institution of Great Britain. 1852) Available at https://www.sgipt.org/medppp/psymot/carp1852.htm [Lasted accessed January 2020]

Carrey, J. "What really exists | under the surface - Jim Carrey" Available at https://www.youtube.com/watch?v=TucyzpHDNlE [Lasted accessed January 2020]

Carrey, J. "Jim and Andy: The Great Beyond | Officiol Trailer [HD] | Netflix" Available at https://www.youtube.com/watch?v=kB15UFO5ebA [Lasted accessed January 2020]

Callender, C. What Makes Time Special? (Oxford University Press. 2017)

Chappelle, D. "COMEDIENS IN CARS GETTING COFFEE. Dave Chappelle." Available at https://www.netflix.com/watch/80171372 [Lasted accessed January 2020]

Csíkszentmihályi, M. "TED 2004. Flow, the secret to happiness." Available at https://www.ted.com/talks/mihaly_csikszentmihalyi_flow_the_secret_to_happiness?language=en#t-342491 [Lasted accessed January 2020]

Davis, P. "Paul Davis – What are Observers?" Available at https://www.youtube.com/watch?v=BzMl_yzcaxo [Lasted accessed January 2021]

Davis, W. "TED 2003. Dreams from endangered cultures." Available at https://www.ted.com/talks/wade_davis_dreams_from_endangered_cultures/transcript?language=en#t-706826 [Lasted accessed January 2020]

Davis, W. "Schooling the world | Wade Davis | TEDxWestVancouverED" Available at https://www.youtube.com/watch?v=hwk2w-9aekA [Last accessed January 2020]

Dawkins, R. "Making Sense Podcast. #174 - LIFE & MIND." Available at https://samharris.org/podcasts/174-life-mind/ [Lasted accessed January 2020]

Dawkins, R. "Why the universe seems so strange" Available at https://www.ted.com/talks/richard_dawkins_why_the_universe_seems_so_strange [Last accessed July 2020]

Dawkins, R. The Extended Phenotype (Oxford University Press. 1982)

Dennett, C. D. "A short guide to your mind" Available at **https://www.bbc.co.uk/programmes/articles/4SMqS8q3sH8hL9DfBrqfzhd/a-short-guide-to-your-mind** [Last accessed July 2020]

Dennett, C. D. Consciousness explained (Little, Brown and Co. 1991)

Dennett, C. D. The Self as a Centre of Narrative Gravity (Lawrence Erlbaum Associates. 1992)

Donaldson, F, O. Playing by Heart: The Vision and Practice of Belonging (Health Communications. 1993)

Donaldson, F, O. "Authentic Play" Available at **https://www.aplayfulpath.com/authentic-play/** [Last accessed July 2020]

Dos Santos RG, Osório FL, Crippa JA, Riba J, Zuardi AW, Hallak JE. Antidepressive, anxiolytic, and antiaddictive effects of ayahuasca, psilocybin and lysergic acid diethylamide (LSD): a systematic review of clinical trials published in the last 25 years. (Ther Adv Psychopharmacol. 2016;6(3):193–213.) Available at **https://doi.org/10.1177/2045125316638008** [Lasted accessed January 2020]

Epictetus and Arrian. Enchiridion. (CreateSpace Independent Publishing Platform. 2017. Originally published on AD c. 125.)

Einstein, A. The Einstein Papers. A Man of Many Parts. (New York Times. 1972)

Einstein, A., Infled, L. The Evolution of Physics (Cambridge University Press. 1938)

Ferguson, K. Comedy and critical thought: Laughter as resistance. (Contemp Polit Theory18, 247-250. 2019) Available at **https://doi.org/10.1057/s41296-018-0243-2**

Feynman, P. W. The Quotable Feynman. (Princeton University Press. 2015)

Gilbert, D. "The surprising science of happiness" Available at **https://www.ted.com/talks/dan_gilbert_the_surprising_science_of_happiness** [Last Accessed July 2020]

Grof, S. LSD Psychotherapy: The Healing Potential of Psychedelic Medicine (Multidisciplinary Association for Psychedelic Studies. 2001. First published 1975)

Griffiths, R. R., Johnson, M. W., Richards, W. A., Richards, B. D., Jesse, R., MacLean, K. A., ... Klinedinst, M. A. (2018). "Psilocybin-occasioned mystical-type experience in combination with meditation and other spiritual practices produces enduring positive changes in psychological functioning and in trait measures of prosocial attitudes and behaviours." *Journal of Psychopharmacology*, *32*(1), 49–69. Available at https://doi.org/10.1177/0269881117731279

Griffiths, R. R., Johnson, M. W., Carducci, M. A., Umbricht, A., Richards, W. A., Richards, B. D., ... Klinedinst, M. A. (2016). Psilocybin produces substantial and sustained decreases in depression and anxiety in patients with life-threatening cancer: A randomized double-blind trial. (Journal of Psychopharmacology, *30*(12), 1181–1197.) Available at https://doi.org/10.1177/0269881116675513

Griffiths, R. R. "Making Sense Podcast, #177 – Psychedelic Science." Available at https://samharris.org/podcasts/177-psychedelic-science/ [Lasted accessed January 2020]

Grotowski, J. Towards a Poor Theatre. (Jaime Soriano. 2009)

Grünau, V. M., Paul A. Kolers, A. P. Shape and color in apparent motion (Elsevier BV. 1976) Available at **https://doi.org/10.1016/0042-6989(76)90192-9**

Harris, S. Free Will (Free Press. 2012)

Harari, N. Y. Sapiens: A Brief History of Humankind (Harper. 2014)

Henry, C. R. The mental Universe. (*Nature* 436, 29. 2005). Available at **https://doi.org/10.1038/436029a** [Lasted accessed January 2020]

Hicks, B. Sane Man (VHS: 1989; DVD: 2005; Netflix as of September 2017)

Hoare, B. "Do swallows return to the same nest?" (BBC Wildlife Magazine) Available at **https://www.discoverwildlife.com/animal-facts/birds/do-swallows-return-to-the-same-nest/** [Lasted accessed January 2020]

Hof, W. "This Trick Makes You Immune To Illness | Wim Hof on Impact Theory" Available at

https://www.youtube.com/watch?v=TM6WKeZ43s4&t=2297s [Last accessed July 2020]

Hoffman, D. D. "Donald Hoffman has a radical new theory on how we experience reality" Available at https://www.ted.com/talks/the_ted_interview_donald_hoffman_has_a_radical_new_theory_on_how_we_experience_reality [Lasted accessed January 2020]

Hoffman, D. D. The Case Against Reality: Why Evolution Hid the Truth from Our Eyes (W. W. Norton Company. 2019)

Hume, D. A Treatise of Human Nature (Hard Press. 2006. Originally published 1740)

Hyde, L. Trickster Makes This World: Mischief, Myth and Art (Farrar, Straus and Giroux. 1997)

James, W. Principles of Psychology (Henry Holt and Company. 1890)

Jeans, J. The Mysterious Universe. (Cambridge University Press. 1930)

Jung, G. C. Civilization in Transition (Collected Works of C. G. Jung) (Routledge. 1964)

Kornhuber, H.H., Deecke, L. Hirnpotentialänderungen bei Willkürbewegungen und passiven Bewegungen des Menschen: Bereitschaftspotential und reafferente Potentiale. Pflügers Arch. 284, 1–17 (1965). **https://doi.org/10.1007/BF00412364** [Last accessed January 2020]

Larkin, P. Collected Poems. (Faber and Faber. 1988)

Libet, B. Unconscious cerebral initiative and the role of conscious will in voluntary action (Behavioural and Brain Sciences. 1985) Available at https://doi.org/10.1017/S0140525X00044903 [Last accessed January 2020]

Marteinson, G. P. On the Problem of the Comic: A Philosophical Study on the Origins of Laughter (Legas. 2006)

Meade, M. "Stories To Safe Us" Available at **https://luminarypodcasts.com/listen/russell-brand/under-the-skin-with-russell-brand/144-stories-to-save-us-with-michael-meade/34d09b1f-8549-4f72-a428-00a74c61789f** [Last accessed September 2020]

Martinez, R. The radical ideas of Raoul Martinez (The Irish Times. 2017)

Martinez, R. Creating Freedom: Power, Control and the Fight for Our Future (Canongate Books. 2016)

McKenna, T. "Terrence McKenna Decribes DMT Trip (rare)" Available at https://www.youtube.com/watch?v=VavdCpewQbA&t=370s [Last accessed January 2020]

Moskowitz, Clara. "Largest Molecules Yet Behave Like Waves in Quantum Double-Slit Experiment". Available at https://www.livescience.com/19268-quantum-double-slit-experiment-largest-molecules.html [Last accessed July 2020]

Oxfam. Reward Work, Not Wealth. (Oxfam.org. 2018) Available at **https://www.oxfamamerica.org/static/media/files/Reward_Work_Not_Wealth_Full_Report_-_English_-_Embargo_22_January_2018.pdf** [Lasted accessed January 2020]

Palhano-Fontes F, Barreto D, Onias H, et al. Rapid antidepressant effects of the psychedelic ayahuasca in treatment-resistant depression: a randomized placebo-controlled trial. *Psychol Med.* 2019;49(4):655–663. **https://doi.org/10.1017/S0033291718001356** [Lasted accessed January 2020]

Sacks, O. Musicophilia: Tales of Music and the Brain. (Knopf. 2007)

Sagan, D. and Margulis, L. Dazzle Gradually: Reflections on the Nature of Nature. (Chelsea Green Publishing Company. 2007)

Schopenhauer, A. Essay on the Freedom of the Will (Dover Publications Inc. 2005. Originally published in 1839)

Spinoza, B. Ethics (Wordsworth Editions Limited. 2001. First published 1677)

Stromer, R. "Shiva Nataraja: A Study in Myth, Iconography, and the Meaning of a Sacred Symbol" Available at https://pdfs.semanticscholar.org/a927/520813b88453309db8d7c4a158f23416cd0d.pdf [Last accessed September 2020]

Subramuniyaswami, S. S. Dancing with Siva Hinduism's Contemporary Catechism (Himalayan Academy. 1991)

Rogan, J. "Joe Rogan: Strange Times" Available at **https://www.netflix.com/watch/80215419** [Last accessed July 2020]

Taylor, B. J. "TED 2008 My Stroke of Insight" Available at **https://www.ted.com/talks/jill_bolte_taylor_my_stroke_of_insight?language=en** [Lasted accessed January 2020]

Tolle, E. The Power of Now (Namaste Publishing. 1997)

Tolle, E. "Become Awake Now! | Eckhart Tolle & Russell Brand - Full Episode" Available at **https://www.youtube.com/watch?v=6EwzvKF-o_Y&t=21s** [Last accessed July 2020]

Uthaug, M.V., van Oorsouw, K., Kuypers, K.P.C. et al. Psychopharmacology (2018) 235: 2979. Sub-acute and long-term effects of ayahuasca on affect and cognitive thinking style and their association with ego dissolution. Available at https://doi.org/10.1007/s00213-018-4988-3 [Lasted accessed January 2020]

Velmans, M. Understanding Consciousness (Routledge. 2000)

Velmans, M. "Max Velmans on "From West towards East in Five Simple Steps"" Available at https://www.youtube.com/watch?v=63QdHwnKf5I [Lasted accessed January 2020]

Wade, K. A. Garry, M. Don Read, J. et al. Psychonomic Bulletin & Review (2002) 9: 597. "A picture is worth a thousand lies: using false photographs to create false childhood memories." (Springer-Verlag. 2002) Available at **https://doi.org/10.3758/BF03196318** [Lasted accessed January 2020]

Watts, A. "Birth, Death and the Unborn." Available at https://www.amazon.com/Birth-Death-Unborn-Pt-1/dp/B07DWCQ4LX?ref_=nav_signin& [Lasted accessed January 2020]

Watts, A. "Alan Watts – The Cosmos" Available at https://www.youtube.com/watch?v=8YdDLHrMMzs&fbclid=IwAR0K-dNvALx5Jxk-3PiphbxTlkWLt1mh1bugqxVPeQoVyigM6q9Ch8rzNQE [Last accessed January 2020]

Watts, A. The Wisdom of Insecurity: A Message for an Age of Anxiety (Vintage. 1968)

Watts, R. "What's in a joke?" Available at **https://www.smh.com.au/entertainment/comedy/whats-in-a-joke-comedians-dissect-comedy-ahead-of-just-for-laughs-20141013-114vmx.html** [Last accessed July 2020]

"What's the point of laughter?" Available at **https://www.sciencefocus.com/the-human-body/whats-the-point-of-laughter/** [Lasted accessed July 2020]

Wheeler, A. J. The 'Past' and the 'Delayed-Choice' Double-Slit Experiment (Elsevier BV. 1978) Available at https://doi.org/10.1016/B978-0-12-473250-6.50006-6 [Last accessed January 2020]

Wolf, A. F. Taking the Quantum Leap: The New Physics for Nonscientists. (Harper Perennial. 1981)

Wilson, A. R. Prometheus Rising. (New Falcon Publications. 1983)

Wilson, A. R. "Maybe Logic : The Lives & Ideas of Robert Anton Wilson (Full Documentary)" Available at https://www.youtube.com/watch?v=2PhHbtBQn44 [Lasted accessed January 2020]

Wiltshire, S. "Billions of Windows – Autistic Savant Artist draws Cities From Memory" Available at **https://www.youtube.com/watch?v=l1O_TMTc660&t=11s** [Last accessed January 2021]

Wittgenstein, L. Tractatus Logico- philosophicus (Routledge Classics. 2001) First published in 1921

Printed in Great Britain
by Amazon

83636566R00142